P9-DNY-157

THE BONDAGE BREAKER

YOUTH EDITION

Neil T. Anderson & Dave Park

HARVEST HOUSE PUBLISHERS
Eugene, Oregon 97402

Cover by Terry Dugan Design, Minneapolis, Minnesota

The names of certain individuals mentioned in this book have been changed in order to protect their privacy.

THE BONDAGE BREAKER YOUTH EDITION
Copyright © 2001 by Harvest House Publishers
Eugene, Oregon 97402

Library of Congress Cataloging-in-Publication Data

Anderson, Neil T., 1942-
The bondage breaker youth edition / Neil T. Anderson, David Park.
p. cm.
ISBN 0-7369-0346-1
1. Christian teenagers—Religious life. 2. Spiritual warfare. I. Park, David, 1961 - II. Title.

BV4531.3 .A53 2001
248.8'3 — dc21   00-053955

Printed in the United States of America.

02 03 04 05 06 07 08 09 10 / BP-MS / 10 9 8 7 6 5 4 3

Acknowledgments

We are so grateful that Harvest House agreed to do a second edition of this book. The message of our freedom in Christ has never been more needed in the lives of young people than today. The hurt, rejection, and bondage that our youth are enduring have a resolution! The answer is Jesus Christ, the Bondage Breaker.

A lot of water has passed under the bridge since *The Bondage Breaker Youth Edition* was first published. We had no idea that this book and *Stomping Out the Darkness* (published by Regal Books) would launch an international youth ministry and prompt dozens of youth books and study guides to be written. Our parent conferences, youth worker conferences, and student conferences have been conducted all over the United States, Canada and around the world!

In the last ten years, we have gained a lot more experience and, we hope, maturity in the Lord. For this reason, we believe this second edition is a much better book than the first edition. The basic message is the same, but now we can say it much better, because it has passed by hundreds of doctoral students, pastors, youth workers, and ministry colleagues. No person has helped us more in this area than our dear friend, Dr. Robert Saucy. Thank you for holding us accountable to the highest standards of biblical integrity. We are indebted to you and so is the body of Christ. It was a great privilege for us to coauthor the youth books *Sold Out for God* and *Higher Ground* with you. It has helped us and thousands of youth to better understand what sanctification is all about.

We want to acknowledge all the awesome students who shared their lives with us. It was a privilege to see God set you free in Christ. There were many emotional moments as we recalled the pain and torment you suffered. We have learned from every one of you as you shared your spiritual journeys with us. How wonderful to see God demonstrate His sufficient grace in your lives.

We also want to acknowledge the youth workers who have labored and shepherded so lovingly in the lives of young sheep. Thank you for your personal sacrifice and commitment to young people! The next step for us at Freedom in Christ Youth Ministries is to certify local youth workers to conduct our parent, youth worker, and student conferences. The message of Freedom in Christ must be multiplied and shared. We feel that no one is better equipped to meet the needs of today's youth than the local church and its shepherds.

Since it was first released less than eight years ago, almost 100,000 students have read *The Bondage Breaker Youth Edition*. What would happen if in *just the next year* a hundred thousand Christian students discovered who they really are in Jesus Christ? What would happen if they turned from sin and truly embraced the freedom that we have in Christ? What would happen if they began to hear the voice of God and actually follow His leading and guidance in their lives with a walk of obedience? The results would be staggering. The results would be revival! Prayer, evangelism, discipleship and multiplication would explode.

We are asking you to not just dream about the possibilities, but to become by God's grace and power the messenger of truth and freedom that students desperately need today. Evangelism and discipleship cannot take place outside an environment of freedom. Join us today in helping students discover the truth that will set them free. Become part of the Freedom in Christ strategies team. In just a few weeks you can be certified to train students, parents, and youth workers using FIC strategies. Thanks again for standing in the gap for our youth!

—Neil and Dave

For more information concerning FIC strategies
training for youth worker or student conferences,
or for FIC strategies resource material,
write to:

Freedom in Christ Youth Ministries
9051 Executive Park Dr., Suite 503
Knoxville, TN 37923
865-342-4000 Phone
865-342-4001 Fax
E-mail: dave@ficm.org
Website: www.ficyouth.com

Contents

Foreword

by Josh McDowell

When I was first asked to write a foreword for *The Bondage Breaker Youth Edition* about ten years ago, I wrote that young people have two absorbing concerns. First, they desperately want to gain some sense of identity. Second, they want to experience the freedom to really walk with God.

If you are a young person, these concerns are just as true for you now as they were for your counterparts ten years ago. And the guidance and truth you will receive from this book are just as relevant today as they were ten years ago because Neil and Dave point you back to the timeless principles of the Word of God. In a day and age when biblical truth is often ignored and many teens are grappling with a basic sense of what is right and what is wrong, it is comforting to know that there are some good voices out there helping you learn who you really are in Christ and how you can break free from the world's bondages. I have shared many times in my speaking and writing about my own personal struggles with poor self-image, and I can say without hesitation that the realization of who I am in Christ is the single most important element in my successful walk as a Christian and in ministry.

Jesus promised that through Him we could live abundant and free lives. And this book, *The Bondage Breaker Youth Edition,* can help you stand against the spiritual forces of this world and live in the freedom He has given. Updated and expanded to address the issues you are facing today, the book deserves your time and careful study. I encourage every young person who desires to walk free and really understand who he or she is in Christ to read it. You'll be glad you did!

Until the whole world hears,
Josh McDowell

Free at Last!

A FEW YEARS AGO I (NEIL) was speaking in a church about the New Age movement. I spoke from 1 Timothy 4:1: "The Spirit explicitly says that in later times some will fall away from the faith, paying attention to deceitful spirits and doctrines of demons." After my message I was surrounded at the front of the sanctuary by hurting people.

Sitting about halfway back in the sanctuary was a 22-year-old woman who had been weeping uncontrollably since the service ended. Several people had tried to comfort her, but she wouldn't allow anyone to get near her. Finally a church staff member cut through the crowd around me and said, "I'm sorry, folks, but we need Dr. Anderson back here right away."

As I approached the young woman, I could hear her sobbing, "He understands! He understands!" We were able to get her out of the sanctuary and into a private office. After she calmed down, I set up a time when we could meet together.

When Nancy arrived for her appointment, her face was marked by ugly, open scratch wounds. "I've been scratching myself like this ever since last week, and I can't control it," she admitted with embarrassment.

Nancy described her horrible childhood, which included an abusive father and a grandmother who identified herself as a black witch. "When I was three years old I received my guardians—spirit guides," she continued. "They were my companions, telling me how to live and what to say. I never questioned whether having spirit guides was anything but normal until my mother took me to Sunday school. Then I began to suspect that my spirit guides might not be good for me. When I asked my parents about it, my father beat me. I never asked again!"

In order to deal with the increasing torment that her spirit guides brought to her life, Nancy resorted to rigid personal discipline. In her high school years she trusted Christ as her Savior. But instead of leaving, her "guardians" continued to harass her.

After high school, Nancy joined the Marines. Determined to become the toughest lady Marine, she won awards for her discipline. But her spiritual torment kept pushing her mind and emotions to the edge. She refused to tell anyone about her mental battle for fear that she would be labeled insane. Finally the pressure overcame her, and she snapped. Nancy quietly accepted a medical discharge and retreated to a lonely existence of inner turmoil and pain. This was her condition when she came to church and heard me talk about deceiving spirits.

"Finally someone understands me!" Nancy said tearfully.

"Would you like to get rid of your spirit guides?" I asked.

There was a long pause. "Will they really leave, or will I go home and be thrashed by them again?"

"You will be free," I assured her.

Two hours later Nancy *was* free—and was hugging us with an openness she had never known before. "Now I can have people over to my house!" she exclaimed joyfully.

The Reality of the Dark Side

Nancy's experience is not uncommon. Although the degree of her problem was somewhat exceptional, we have come to realize that Paul had in mind every believer when he wrote, "Our struggle is not against flesh and blood, but against the rulers, against the powers, against the world forces of this darkness, against the spiritual forces of wickedness in the heavenly places" (Ephesians 6:12). We have ministered to thousands of young Christians all over the world who are being deceived and are living defeated lives. This is a real tragedy, because their heavenly Father desires for them to live a free and productive life in Christ.

Our journey into this realm of ministry did not come by choice. We were never curious about demon activity or the occult. The lure of knowledge and occultic power never appealed to us.

On the other hand, we have always been disposed to believe what the Bible says about the spiritual world, even when it seems to conflict with the Western worldview. As a result, the Lord has been bringing Christians like Nancy to see us. They have been dominated by thought patterns, habits, and behaviors that have kept them from living free and full lives.

Through years of learning and ministering, we have a better understanding of how the truth sets us free and of the need to resist the devil as well as submit to God (James 4:7). Ministries that ignore the reality of the spiritual world don't have an adequate answer, but neither do some deliverance ministries that see the problem as only spiritual. God is reality, and He relates to us as whole people—and His Word provides the total answer for all those who live in this fallen world.

God Wants You Free and Growing in Christ

Since the first release of this book, we have coauthored (with Dr. Robert Saucy) two books on sanctification, entitled *Sold*

Out for God and *Higher Ground* (published by Harvest House). Understanding the process of sanctification (being set apart for God's special purpose) is critical since God's will for our lives is our sanctification (1 Thessalonians 4:3). "We will in all things grow up into him who is the Head, that is, Christ...and become mature, attaining to the whole measure of the fullness of Christ" (Ephesians 4:15,13 NIV). If God has given us everything we need to mature in Christ (2 Peter 1:3), then why aren't more Christians growing in Christ? Some young believers are no more Christlike now than they were five or ten years ago. Paul says, "The goal of our instruction is love from a pure heart and a good conscience and a sincere faith" (1 Timothy 1:5). Every year of our Christian life, we should be able to say, "I have grown in my faith, and now I love God and others more this year than I did last year." If we can't say that, then we are not growing.

Part of the reason for this immaturity and worldliness is given in 1 Corinthians 3:2,3: "I gave you milk to drink, not solid food; for you were not yet able to receive it. Indeed, even now you are not yet able, for you are still fleshly. For since there is jealousy and strife among you, are you not fleshly, and are you not walking like mere men?" According to Paul, some Christians are not even able to receive good teaching from the Bible because of unresolved conflicts in their lives. What is needed is some way to resolve these personal and spiritual conflicts through genuine repentance and faith in God. That is the purpose of this book.

In our first book, *Stomping Out the Darkness* (published by Regal Books), we focused more on the personal side of the young believer's life in Christ and walk by faith. That book deals with the foundational issues of your identity in Christ and outlines practical steps on how to live by faith, walk according to the Spirit, renew your mind, manage your emotions, and resolve the emotional problems of your past through faith and forgiveness. (To see the complete picture, we strongly suggest that you read *Stomping Out the Darkness* as well as this book. Either book can be accompanied by the video or audiotape series by Dave entitled *Busting Free,* which may be purchased from the office of Freedom in Christ Ministries.)

Before we received Christ, we were slaves to sin. But because of what Christ did on the cross, sin's power over us has been broken. Satan no longer owns us, and he has no right to tell us what to do. He is a defeated foe, but he is committed to keeping us from realizing that. The father of lies can block your victory as a Christian if he can deceive you into believing that you are nothing but a product of your past—ruled by sin, stuck in the failure mode, and controlled by your habits.

Paul said, "It was for freedom that Christ set us free; therefore keep standing firm and do not be subject again to a yoke of slavery" (Galatians 5:1). You are free in Christ, but you will be defeated if the devil can fool you into believing you are nothing more than a sin-sick product of your past. Nor can Satan do anything about your position in Christ, but if he can deceive you into believing what the Scripture says isn't true, you will live as though it isn't. People are in bondage to the lies they believe. That is why Jesus said, "You will know the truth, and the truth will make you free" (John 8:32).

We don't believe in instant maturity. It will take us the rest of our lives to renew our minds and be conformed to the image of God (Romans 12:1). But it doesn't take long to help young people resolve their personal and spiritual issues and find their freedom in Christ. Being alive and free in Christ is part of *positional* sanctification, which is the basis for *progressive* sanctification. In other words, we are not trying to

become children of God, we *are* children of God who are
becoming like Christ. (Again, to learn more about sanctification, check out *Sold Out for God* and *Higher Ground*.)
Once people are established alive and free in Christ through
real repentance and faith in God, watch them grow! They
have a new thirst for the Word of God, and they know who
they are in Christ because "the Spirit Himself testifies with
our spirit that we are children of God" (Romans 8:16).

In this book we want to describe the spiritual battle that
we are in and how young Christians can find their victory in
Christ. Part One explains your position of freedom, protection, and authority in Christ. Part Two warns of your vul-
nerability to temptation, accusation, and deception. Part
Three presents the Steps to Freedom in Christ, which will
enable you to submit to God and resist the devil (James 4:7).

Are you perhaps one of those Christians who lives in
bondage to fear, depression, habits you can't break, thoughts
or inner voices you can't get away from, or sinful behavior
you can't escape? God has made every provision for you to
be alive and free in Christ. Throughout these pages we want
to introduce you to the One who has already overcome the
darkness and secured your freedom: Jesus Christ, the
Bondage Breaker!

Part 1

Take Courage!

You Don't Have to Live in the Shadows

ONE

I (NEIL) REMEMBER COUNSELING a young Christian who was in deep spiritual, mental, and emotional confusion. At one point before I began meeting with her, she wrote the following prayer, then ten minutes later tried unsuccessfully to kill herself with an overdose of pills:

> Dear God,
>
> Where are you? How can you watch and not help me? I hurt so bad, and you don't even care. If you cared you'd make it stop or let me die. I love you, but you seem so far away. I can't hear you or feel you or see you, but I'm supposed to believe you're here. Lord, I feel them and hear them. They are here. I know you're real, God, but they are more real to me right now. Please make someone believe me, Lord. Why won't you make it stop? Please, Lord, please! If you love me you'll let me die.
>
> —A Lost Sheep

We have met hundreds of young Christians like the one who wrote this sad note. Most of them didn't attempt suicide as this one did, but many of them talked about dark desires to do so. And nearly all of them admitted to the presence of "them"—inner urges or voices that bothered them, tempted and taunted them, accused them, or threatened them.

The fact that people struggle with negative or opposing thoughts is well accepted. We often caution young people who make appointments to talk with us that they may have opposing thoughts such as, "Don't go; they can't help you." Or distracting thoughts will pop into their minds, such as, "I don't want to go" or "I've tried this before and it didn't work." One person wrote to Neil: "Every time I try to talk to you, or even think about talking to you, I completely shut down. Voices inside literally yell at me: 'No!' I've even considered killing myself to end this terrible battle going on inside. I need help!"

Over the years, wherever we go we have surveyed Christian high school students, asking them "Have you heard 'voices' in your head like there was a subconscious self talking to you, or have you struggled with really bad thoughts?" Seventy percent answered yes! If you struggle with tempting or accusing thoughts in your head, you're not alone. You may not have told anyone about your experiences because you fear that people would think you're a mental case. Maybe you have kept quiet because *you* think you're crazy. Maybe you have been taught that Christians can't have these kinds of problems.

But the time has come for us to wake up to the fact that Satan is real and that demons exist. If you hear tormenting voices in your head or feel a dark presence in your room at night (and 47 percent of those students we've surveyed have), you're not crazy; you're under attack. You need to know how to defend yourself against Satan's fiery darts. That's what this book is all about.

Many Christians don't complain about hearing voices, but their minds are filled with such confusion that their daily walk with Christ is completely discouraging. When they try to pray, they begin thinking about a million things they should be doing. When they sit down to read the Bible or a good Christian book, they can't concentrate. When they have an opportunity to serve the Lord in some way, they give up because of thoughts of self-doubt: "I'm not a strong Christian"; "I don't know enough about the Bible"; "I'm too young"; "I have too many sinful thoughts." Instead of being victorious, dynamic Christians full of joy, they trudge through life under a cloud, just trying to hang on until Jesus comes. Some of this discouragement is certainly because of our own faulty thinking, but it can also reflect deception from the enemy.

Common Misconceptions About Bondage

Where do the evil voices, bad thoughts, guilty feelings, and confusion come from? One of the main reasons so many youth are in bondage today is because they don't know the answers to these questions. They are living under a number of misconceptions about the spiritual world that must be corrected. Here is what some Christians falsely believe—and Satan loves it.

1. *Demons were busy when Christ was on earth, but they're not around much today.* Young Christians who believe this after reading what God's Word says and seeing what is going on in the world today are not facing the facts. The New Testament clearly says that believers will wrestle "against the rulers, against the powers, against the world forces of this

darkness, against the spiritual forces of wickedness in the heavenly places" (Ephesians 6:12). Paul goes on to describe every piece of spiritual armor we are to put on in order to defend ourselves against "the flaming arrows of the evil one" (verses 13-17). If dark spiritual powers are no longer attacking believers, why would Paul warn us about them and insist that we arm ourselves against them?

The powers and forces that Paul wrote about are still around today. You can see it around your school. How many kids do you know who are involved in New Age practices, Ouija boards, astrology, occult games like Magic, or music with evil lyrics?

The kingdom of darkness is still present, and Satan wants to make our lives miserable and keep us from walking strong and tall in Christ. If you don't believe that Satan and his demons are present and busy, then either God or you will have to take a bum rap for all the evil Satan is dumping on you and the rest of the world.

2. *What early Christians called demonic activity is only mental illness.* If one of your friends were to report hearing inner voices or sensing a dark presence in his room, most secular counselors would say, "He has a mental problem; he's paranoid." Very few would think it's a spiritual problem, the activity of Satan's demons. Why? Because a natural explanation is the best such counselors can do without a belief in God or the existence of Satan. The secular world's understanding of our problems is simply incomplete. It ignores the reality of the spiritual world.

Not all physical, mental, and emotional problems young Christians experience are specifically demonic. But ignoring the presence and influence of Satan and his demons will leave many problems unsolved.

3. *Some problems are psychological and some are spiritual.*
This false belief suggests that the human soul and spirit are
separate, which isn't true. There is no problem that isn't psychological, because there is never a time when our mind,
emotions, and will are not involved. And there is no problem
that isn't spiritual, because there is no time when God is not
present or when it is safe for us to take off the armor of God.

Saying that a problem is only psychological overlooks
how God and Satan are involved. Saying that a problem is
only spiritual ignores our responsibility for how we must
think, feel, and choose. In order to deal with our inner conflicts we must consider both the psychological and spiritual
influences that are at work.

4. *Christians can't be affected by demonic forces.* This is a lie
that the devil would love us to swallow so we will drop our
defenses against him. If Satan can't touch Christians, why are
we told to put on the armor of God, to resist the devil, to stand
firm, and to be alert? If we can't be deceived by Satan, why
does Paul talk about our relationship to the powers of darkness as a wrestling match? Those who say the enemy can't
influence us are the ones who are most vulnerable to him.

5. *The activity of demons is only seen in weird behavior or
gross sin.* There are still cases of demon activity today like
the wild demon-possessed man called "Legion" in Luke 8:26-
39. But most young Christians under spiritual attack lead
fairly normal lives while experiencing serious inner problems for which no natural cause or solution has been found.
Because they think that satanic attack is involved only in the
cases of only mass murderers or violent sex criminals, these
ordinary people wonder what's wrong with them and why
they can't just "do better."

Satan's first and best strategy is deception. Paul warned:
"Satan disguises himself as an angel of light. Therefore it is

not surprising if his servants also disguise themselves as servants of righteousness" (2 Corinthians 11:14,15). It is not the few weird or violent people who are the main problem. Rather, it is Satan's subtle deception and invasion of the lives of "normal" believers like us that keeps us from being effective.

6. *Freedom from spiritual bondage is the result of a power encounter with demonic forces.* Freedom from spiritual problems and bondage does not result from a power encounter; it results from a *truth* encounter. Satan is a liar, and he will work undercover at all costs. But the truth of God's Word exposes him and his lies. His demons are like cockroaches that scurry for the shadows when the light comes on. Satan's power is in the lie, and when his lie is exposed by the truth, his plans are foiled. Satan's power was broken at the cross. He is a defeated foe.

Then how can he be so effective? Let me illustrate with a story from childhood.

When I (Neil) was a boy growing up in the country, my dad, my brother, and I would visit our neighbor's farm. The neighbor had a yappy little dog that scared the socks off me. When it came barking around the corner, my dad and brother stood their ground, but I ran. Guess who the dog chased! I escaped to the top of our pickup truck while the little dog yapped at me from the ground.

Everyone except me could see that the little dog had no power over me except what I gave it by not standing up to it. The dog had no power to throw me up on the pickup; it was my belief that put me up there. That dog controlled me by using my mind, my emotions, my will, and my muscles, all of which were motivated by fear. Finally I gathered up my courage, jumped off the pickup, and kicked a small rock at the mutt. And it ran!

Satan is like that yappy little dog: He deceives us into fearing him more than God. His power is in the lie. He is the father of lies (John 8:44) who deceives the whole world (Revelation 12:9). As a result, the whole world is under the influence of the evil one (1 John 5:19).

The devil can do nothing about who you are in Christ. But if he can deceive you into believing his lies about you and God, you will spend a lot of time on top of the pickup truck! You don't have to outshout him or outmuscle him to be free of his control. You just have to *out-truth* him. *Believe, declare, and act upon the truth of God's Word*, and you will ruin Satan's strategy.

This concept has had a dramatic effect on our counseling. Often when a spiritual conflict was exposed in someone being counseled, it would turn into a power encounter. The person would become unconscious, run out of the room, or start behaving like he or she was crazy. Our usual first approach was to get the demon to expose itself, then command it to leave. This process was often very difficult for the person we were trying to help. And though progress was made, the process would usually have to be repeated.

We have learned from the Bible and from our experience that *truth* is what sets people free. The power of Satan is in the lie, and the power of the believer is in knowing the truth. We are to pursue the truth that sets us free.

Also, people who are in bondage are not liberated by what the counselor does but by what *they* do. It's not what Neil or Dave or your pastor or youth leader believes that breaks Satan's grip on your life, it's what *you* believe. And what you believe must be the truth. Notice the following verses:

> You will know the truth, and the truth will set you free (John 8:32 NIV).
>
> [Jesus said,] "I am the way, and the truth, and the life" (John 14:6).

> When He, the Spirit of truth, comes, He will guide you into all the truth (John 16:13).

> [Jesus prayed to the Father,] "I'm not asking you to take them [Christians] out of the world, but to keep them safe from Satan's power....Make them pure and holy through teaching them your words of truth" (John 17:15,17 TLB).

> Stand firm then, with the belt of truth buckled around your waist (Ephesians 6:14 NIV).

> Finally, brethren, whatever is true...let your mind dwell on these things (Philippians 4:8).

When God first disciplined the early church, as recorded in Acts 5, He did so in a dramatic way. Two people dropped dead when their sin was discovered. What was the issue: drugs, sex? No, the issue was *truth*. Peter confronted Ananias and Sapphira: "Why has Satan filled your heart to lie to the Holy Spirit?" (verse 3). God wanted the church to know that Satan the deceiver can ruin us if he can get us to believe and live a lie. That's why it is so important to take "every thought captive to the obedience of Christ" (2 Corinthians 10:5).

Setting Captives Free

Before Jesus died on the cross and rose from the dead, God empowered Him and His hand-picked disciples to take authority over demonic powers in the world. But something radical happened at the cross and in the resurrection that permanently changed the way we encounter spiritual forces.

First, Jesus' death and resurrection defeated and disarmed the rulers and authorities of the kingdom of darkness (Colossians 2:15). Before the cross, "all authority...in heaven and on earth" had not yet been given to Christ. But Matthew

28:18 assures us that the resurrected Christ now has all authority. Because of the cross, Satan is defeated, and he has no authority over those who are in Christ. Believing the truth of Christ's victory and Satan's defeat is the first step to successfully putting down the enemy's attempts to discourage and hassle you.

Second, in Christ's death and resurrection every believer is made alive with Him and is now seated with Him (Ephesians 2:5,6). You no longer need someone else—like a pastor or youth leader—to take authority over Satan for you. You now reside in Jesus Christ, who has all authority. In order to resist the devil, you need to understand and exercise your position and authority in Christ.

Freedom is your inheritance as a Christian. That's why Paul wrote:

> I pray that your hearts will be flooded with light so that you can see something of the future he has called you to share. I want you to realize that God has been made rich because we who are Christ's have been given to him! I pray that you will begin to understand how incredibly great his power is to help those who believe him. It is the same mighty power that raised Christ from the dead and seated him in the place of honor at God's right hand in heaven, far, far above any other king or ruler or dictator or leader. Yes, his honor is far more glorious than that of anyone else either in this world or the world to come (Ephesians 1:18-21 TLB).

When Satan harasses you, you may want to crawl under a rock in misery, like the girl whose prayer note opened this chapter. You may cry out for God to deliver you, like Jesus miraculously and instantly delivered the demonized people in the Gospels. But your deliverance has already been accomplished because of Christ's work on the cross and His resurrection. That's the good news Paul was trying to tell us about in his prayer. Since you are with Christ in the light, you never again need to live in the shadows.

But it is your responsibility to choose the truth and resist the devil. From your position in Christ, you must resist the devil, renounce (which means to turn your back on) any ways by which you have participated in his schemes, confess your sin, and forgive those who have offended you. These critical Steps to Freedom in Christ are the focus of Part Three of this book.

The woman who called herself "A Lost Sheep" in the letter at the beginning of this chapter finally gained God's view of her condition. Four years after she wrote her desperate prayer, she wrote this response based on her new understanding of God's provision for her in Christ. Her words are based on Scripture. Allow them to shine some light into the shadows of your life.

> My Dear Lost Sheep,
>
> You ask me where I am. My child, I am with you and I always will be. You are weak, but in me you are strong. I love you so much that I can't let you die. I am so close that I feel everything you feel.
>
> I know what you are going through, for I am going through it with you. But I have set you free and you must stand firm. You do not need to die physically for my enemies to be gone, but be crucified with me and I will live in you, and you shall live with me. I will direct you in paths of righteousness. My child, I love you and I will never forsake you, for you are truly mine.
>
> —Love, God

Truth Encounter

Read:

John 8:32; John 14:6; John 16:13

Reflect:

1. Could you relate to the Christians in this chapter who felt spiritually oppressed? What experiences have you had?

2. Have you been exposed to any of the misconceptions talked about in this chapter? Did you accept any of them as true? How did those misconceptions affect your life?

3. Do you feel you fully understand how to use your authority in Christ and resist the devil? What are some ways you can learn more about your authority in Christ?

4. Do you ever feel that your personal walk with Christ is incomplete or that you're not growing? In what ways?

Respond:

Take a few moments to pray, and ask the Lord to reveal to your mind any misconceptions that you might have about bondages or the spiritual world around us. Ask the Lord to replace any deceptions you might have with His truth. Ask Him to help you grow in your understanding of who you are in Christ.

Finding Your Way in the World

IN HIGH SCHOOL I (DAVE) read William Golding's chilling novel, *Lord of the Flies*. Perhaps you have read it in an English or literature class. The book is about a group of boys stranded on an island without adult supervision. They start out treating each other with kindness and respect as they were taught. But eventually the evil side of their nature takes control, resulting in hatred, violence, and even murder.

The book's title is actually taken from a biblical reference to Satan. Beelzebub, one of Satan's names in the Bible, literally means "lord of the flies." This is one of the most descriptive titles for the devil in Scripture. Satan is like a pesky, disease-carrying fly, out to harass and infect every believer with his temptations, accusations, and lies.

This picture of Satan was strongly impressed on my wife, Grace, and me one summer when we returned home after a three-week trip. Our first clue that something was very wrong came when we opened the front door and a swarm of flies came buzzing out. The flies were followed by a strong smell that smacked us square in the face. It was obvious that something inside was very dead.

By the time we reached the kitchen, we were gagging from the smell. And there on the floor in front of our freezer was the source. Somehow the freezer door had come open, and a frozen chicken had fallen out. The rotten bird was nearly twice its original size, and it pulsed and bubbled as if it were alive. During the three weeks we were gone the chicken had thawed and had been transformed into a maternity hospital for flies. When I tried to scoop up the smelly carcass with a dustpan, it burst open and thousands of squirmy maggots spilled out onto the floor. We almost passed out!

This gross picture illustrates what Satan is like. He swarms around people who are spiritually dead or living out of harmony with God. He plants his lies in our minds, and if we don't resist him with the truth, his evil ideas eat away at us like maggots, tearing us down.

Golding would have us believe that the "lord of the flies" is the evil, beastly side of human nature, not Satan, the being who rules the dark side of the spiritual world. Satan would like us to believe he doesn't really exist and evil is just a human weakness. In fact, Satan doesn't want us to believe that the spiritual world exists at all.

But Golding's picture of evil is incomplete. We have three very present and personal enemies: the evil influences of the world, the flesh (our tendency to run our own lives without God), and—most overlooked today—the devil. Satan is a real but unseen being. He and his demons are alive and active in our world today. But, as illustrated by William Golding's novel, he has been very successful in convincing people that *they* are evil and that *he*, the evil one, doesn't exist.

While Christians have been questioning the reality of Satan and the influence of demons, many people have charged full speed into the dark side of the spiritual world.

The New Age movement teaches that we are gods and can create reality with our minds. New Age channelers (who are really spiritual mediums) can be heard on radio and TV talk shows bragging about their spirit guides (which are really demons).

Parapsychology (study of the occult) is becoming accepted as a "science" in our universities. Fascination with the supernatural continues to grow, as seen in the popularity of movies like *Mummy* and *The Sixth Sense*. Even the old film *The Exorcist* was rereleased. The seductive power of Satanism is increasingly evident in our culture.

Fascination with the supernatural is growing even in our Christian schools. Twenty-six percent of the Christian high-schoolers we surveyed have played with a Ouija board, 20 percent have tried astrology, 16 percent have played Dungeons & Dragons, and 12 percent have had their palms read.

Curiosity about the occult and the lure of supernatural knowledge and power has trapped many in Satan's web. To avoid this trap, we must understand this world from God's perspective.

The Two-Level Worldview

What is your worldview? Maybe you've never heard that term before. A worldview is how you understand the world around you and how you relate to it. In other words, a worldview is like a pair of glasses through which you see what is happening in the world. Your worldview is what you believe about reality.

The Western world (North America and parts of Western Europe) sees reality in two levels (see Figure 2a). The upper level is the hidden, unseen world that is understood through religion and spiritual experiences. The lower level is the natural world that is understood through science and the physical senses.

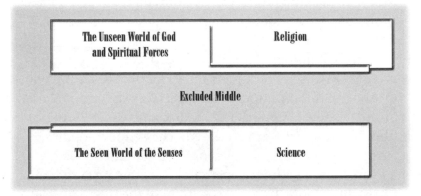

Figure 2a

Those of us educated in the West have been taught that the spiritual, unseen world has no practical effect on the natural world. It has been left out from our understanding of reality. We have been taught to trust only that which we can see, hear, touch, taste, smell, and measure in a laboratory. Many people ignore, doubt, or laugh at the idea of evil spirits having an impact on us. Some others may say they believe in God, but they see Him as uninvolved with human affairs.

In contrast to us in the West, two-thirds of the people of the world hold an Eastern worldview. They believe that spiritual forces are an everyday reality. These people please their gods with peace offerings and perform religious rituals to ward off evil spirits. To the common people in many Third World nations, religious practice or superstition is more practical in daily life than is science.

It is easy for those of us raised in the West to say the Eastern worldview is wrong because of all the "success" of the Western world. *But both are worldly systems, and neither reflects what the Bible says is real.*

Dr. Paul Hiebert, a missions expert, has called this Western separation between the natural and the spiritual the "excluded middle." He believes that spiritual forces are active in the physical world. We must include the spiritual world, including the kingdom of darkness, in our worldview—because in reality there is no excluded middle!

To show how this two-level thinking has affected the beliefs of some Western Christians, let me (Neil) tell you about a bright young woman named Dee, a pastor's daughter. Dee developed physical symptoms that were later diagnosed as multiple sclerosis. When I heard about Dee's condition and the prospect of her life with this crippling disease, I looked for an opportunity to talk to her.

"When did you first become aware of the symptoms?" I asked.

"Right after a special time of devotions I had with the Lord," Dee replied.

"What was so special about your devotions that day?"

"I was feeling sorry for myself, when I read the passage where Paul told about his thorn in the flesh. Paul said God's power was perfected in his weakness, and I wanted God's power in my life too. So I asked for a thorn in the flesh."

"You asked God for a thorn in the flesh?" I tried to hide my shock.

"Yes."

"Do you know what Paul's thorn in the flesh was?"

"Some sort of physical problem, wasn't it?"

"Well, we're not told how it showed itself, but 2 Corinthians 12:7 clearly states that it was an angel of Satan—a demon! Paul never asked for it. In fact, he prayed three times that it be removed. Dee, I think Satan took advantage of your unscriptural prayer and afflicted you with these symptoms. I strongly recommend that you renounce your request for a thorn in the flesh and pray that any influence by Satan be removed from your life."

Dee received my counsel, and we prayed together. She began to feel better almost immediately. The symptoms disappeared, and she resumed her normal activities. Several months later, the symptoms began to reappear. At that time I led her more thoroughly through the Steps to Freedom (see Part Three of this book). Today Dee is free.

Dee's father's first reaction to her illness was typical of many Western Christians who look only for a natural explanation: "I never even considered Dee's condition to be a spiritual problem." For the same reason, some people would argue that Dee's "recovery" was remission of a physical disease instead of freedom from demonic activity.

Many Christians either exclude the supernatural from their worldview or believe that it has no effect on their lives. By doing so they exclude God's power from their beliefs and practices. They also try to explain all human problems— even those brought about by demonic influence, such as Dee's symptoms—as the result of mental or physical causes.

Living in the Excluded Middle

The Christian worldview looks at life through the Bible, not through culture or experience. The Bible clearly teaches that supernatural, spiritual forces are at work in the natural world. For example, approximately one-fourth of all the healings talked about in the Gospel of Mark were actually deliverances from demonic activity. The woman whom Jesus healed in Luke 13:11-13 had been the victim of a "sickness caused by a spirit" for 18 years.

In addition to Dee many other people we have counseled came to us with physical problems that disappeared shortly after the demonic influence was dealt with. The most common physical symptoms we have seen are headaches, dizziness, inability to read and concentrate on the Word of God, and general pain throughout the body.

We're not saying that everyone who is ill or in pain is being terrorized by a demon. That's going overboard toward the unseen spiritual level. But some Christians battle physical symptoms unsuccessfully through natural means when the basic problems and solutions are spiritual. By all means, go see your doctor who will test and treat you physically, *and* see your pastor who should be able to help you spiritually.

Jesus left us "in the world" (John 17:11) to wrestle against "spiritual forces of wickedness in the heavenly places" (Ephesians 6:12). We live in the natural world, but we are involved in a spiritual war. The excluded middle exists only in our worldly minds, not in reality.

Getting Spiritual Without God

Young people in the West have begun to sense that there is more to life than what natural science has revealed. On the surface, this new hunger may sound encouraging to those of us with a Christian worldview. But many youth who are unsatisfied by the materialistic world are often unhappy with organized religion. Instead of turning to Christ and His church, they are trying to fill their spiritual emptiness with the occult, parapsychology, Eastern religions, and numerous cults marching under the banner of the New Age movement.

Trying to meet spiritual needs apart from God is nothing new. The center of this unbiblical worldview is self: What will *I* get out of this? Who will meet *my* needs? I'm doing *my own* thing. Even a Christian who acts this way is motivated by selfish ambition and pride.

The apostle Peter is a clear example of the struggle between self- and Christ-centered living. Only moments after Peter confessed the all-important truth that Jesus Christ is the Messiah, the Son of the living God (Matthew 16:13-16), he found himself taking sides with the powers of darkness. When Jesus announced that suffering and death awaited Him at Jerusalem, "Peter took Him aside and began to rebuke Him, saying, 'God forbid it, Lord! This shall never happen to You'" (verse 22).

Jesus responded: "Get behind Me, Satan! You are a stumbling block to Me; for you are not setting your mind on God's interests, but man's" (verse 23).

Jesus' put-down seems cold and severe. But His remark clearly describes the nature of the advice Peter tried to give: "Save yourself at all costs. Watch out for yourself. Don't do anything that is painful or inconvenient."

Peter's advice was from Satan, for Satan's primary aim is to get us all to center our lives on our own interests. But the Christian worldview has a different center. Jesus confronts our self-serving motives and offers the view from the cross. Only from this perspective can we escape the bondage of Satan, whose sole intent is "to steal and kill and destroy" (John 10:10).

The View from the Cross

Together with his wife Eve, Adam was the first human to entertain the idea that he could "be like God" (Genesis 3:5), which is the core of the self-centered worldview that Satan promotes. Countless others since Adam have been tempted by Satan into believing that they are their own gods, and today the New Age movement is promoting this lie in a big way.

However, the biblical account of creation clearly shows us that only God the Creator is truly God. Adam and his ancestors are not gods; we are created beings who cannot live apart from God. The idea that people are their own gods is the heartbeat of the Satan-inspired worldview and the primary link in the chain of spiritual bondage to the kingdom of darkness.

The problem with our attempt to be our own gods is that we were never designed to be gods. We lack the needed qualities to take care of our own lives and futures. Even sinless, spiritually alive Adam in the garden of Eden wasn't equipped to be his own god, much less those of us born since then, who come into the world spiritually dead. Contrary to what the New Agers tell us, the ability to be a god never was in us, isn't in us now, and never will be in us. Being God is something that belongs to God alone.

If you desire to live in freedom from the bondage of the world, the flesh, and the devil, this important link in the chain must be smashed. The self-centered worldview that Satan and his demons are promoting all around you must be replaced by the teachings of Jesus. We must understand what Jesus taught His disciples after Peter's self-preserving rebuke:

> If anyone wants to be a follower of mine, let him deny himself and take up his cross and follow me. For anyone who keeps his life for himself shall lose it; and anyone who loses his life for me shall find it again. What profit is there if you gain the whole world—and lose eternal life? What can be compared to the value of eternal life? For I, the Son of Mankind, shall come with my angels in the glory of my Father and judge each person according to his deeds (Matthew 16:24-27 TLB).

The following six guidelines from Jesus' statement make up the view from the cross. They are the needed guidelines for those young Christians who want to be free from the bondage of the world system and the devil who inspires it. Stay within the light of the victory of the cross, and you will successfully find your way in a dark world.

Deny Yourself

Denying yourself is not the same as self-denial. All athletes practice self-denial, restricting themselves from certain foods, drugs, alcohol, all-night parties, and anything else that keeps them from reaching their goals. But the ultimate purpose of self-denial is self-promotion: to win a game, to break a record, to achieve athletic status and recognition.

Jesus was talking about denying yourself in the struggle over who is going to be God in your life. Jesus doesn't enter into that battle; He's already won it. He occupies the throne and graciously offers to share it with us. But we want to be king in our lives. Until we deny ourselves that which was never meant to be ours—the role of being God in our lives—we will never be at peace with ourselves or God, and we will never be free.

You were not designed to function without God, nor was your soul designed to work as your own master. You will either serve God and His kingdom or Satan and his kingdom. When you deny yourself, you invite God to take the throne of your life, to occupy what is rightfully His, so that you may live as a person who is spiritually alive in Christ. Denying yourself is essential to spiritual freedom.

Pick Up Your Cross Daily

The cross we are to pick up on a daily basis is not our *own* cross but *Christ's* cross. It is His cross that we are closely identified with. Paul wrote, "I have been crucified with Christ; and it is no longer I who live, but Christ lives in me; and the life which I now live in the flesh I live by faith in the Son of God, who loved me and gave Himself up for me" (Galatians 2:20). His cross provided forgiveness from what we have done and deliverance from what we were. We are forgiven because He died in our place; we are delivered because we died with Him. We are both justified (made acceptable to God) and sanctified (set apart for a holy purpose) as a result of the cross.

To pick up the cross daily means to realize every day that we belong to God. We have been purchased by the blood of the Lord Jesus Christ (1 Peter 1:18,19). When we pick up the cross, we are saying that our identity and purpose is not based in our physical life but in our relationship with God.

Follow Christ

We follow Christ by being led by the Holy Spirit to the death of self-rule. As Paul wrote: "We who are alive are constantly being given over to death for Jesus' sake, so that his life may be revealed in our mortal body" (2 Corinthians 4:11 NIV).

You might be thinking, "Dying to self-rule doesn't sound like fun to me. In fact, it sounds awful." Well, it's not. It is a tremendous victory (and a tremendous relief for us) when we stop trying to play God and let God be the Lord of our lives, our problems, and our future. Being led by the Spirit of God is our assurance that we are His children (Romans 8:14). Only when we come to the end of our resources do we discover God's resources.

We were not designed to function independently of God. Only when we are dependent on Him and intent on following Christ are we complete and free to prove that the will of God is good, acceptable, and perfect (Romans 12:2). "Deny yourself, pick up your cross daily, and follow Me" may seem like you are sacrificing yourself and gaining nothing. Nothing could be further from the truth, for what are you really sacrificing?

Sacrifice the Lower Life to Gain the Higher Life

If you want to save your natural life (in other words, find your identity and sense of self-worth in positions, titles, accomplishments, and possessions, and seek only worldly well-being), you will lose it. At best you can possess these things of earthly value only for a lifetime—but you will lose everything for eternity. Furthermore, in all your efforts to possess these earthly treasures, you will fail to gain all that can be yours in Christ.

I (Dave) received a letter from a teenager who made this important discovery:

> Dear Dave,
>
> In our conversation about my grades in sociology and chemistry, you said something that really made me think. You said, "Don't let it be pride." At first I felt offended. Why? Because I had believed so thoroughly that grades would bring me worth. I believed this so much that I had taken grades and let them become a god to me. I thought that good grades could be my defense against my insecurities. I felt I was good enough because of my grades.
>
> After talking with you I realized I was deceiving myself. I wasn't walking in the Spirit. Now I know that it's God, not my grades, who makes me secure, accepted, and significant. If I am honestly humble, *He* will lift me up and reward me.

Shoot for this world and that's all you'll get, and eventually you will lose even that. But shoot for the next world and God will throw in this one as a bonus. Paul made a similar statement: "Bodily discipline is only of little profit, but godliness is profitable for all things, since it holds promise for the present life and also for the life to come" (1 Timothy 4:8).

Sacrifice the Pleasure of Things to Gain the Pleasure of Life

What would you accept in trade for the fruit of the Spirit in your life? What material possession, what amount of money, what position or title would you take in exchange for the love, joy, peace, and patience (Galatians 5:22) that you can have if you abide in Christ? "Nothing," we would all probably agree. The lie of this world is that fame and possessions will bring us the fruit of the Spirit. Where is the majority of our time and energy being spent: on temporary things or eternal things? It seems to be the great ambition of man to be happy as animals instead of being blessed as children of God.

Jesus talked about this very conflict with two of His closest friends, Mary and Martha (Luke 10:38-42). During Jesus' visit, Martha was caught up in material things, focusing on preparing and serving a meal, while Mary centered her attention on Jesus and His words. Martha's tendency was to love things and use people, but Jesus indicated that Mary had chosen "the good part" (verse 42) by loving people and using things. Victory over self comes as we learn to love people and use things, and not get those two activities mixed up.

Sacrifice the Temporary to Gain the Eternal

Possibly the greatest sign of spiritual maturity is the ability to postpone rewards. The flesh wants instant gratification, but the more you try to satisfy its lusts, the less hope you have for the future. The more you feed a lust, the larger it grows, and you will end up sacrificing the eternal to gain the temporal. Hebrews 11:24-26 says: "By faith Moses, when he had grown up, refused to be called the son of Pharaoh's daughter, choosing rather to endure ill-treatment with the people of God than to enjoy the passing pleasures of sin, considering the reproach of Christ greater riches than the treasures of Egypt; for he was looking to the reward." Even if following Christ results in tough times in this life, He will make it right in eternity.

Satan's ultimate lie is that you are capable of being the god of your own life, and bondage is living as though his lie were true. Satan is out to take God's place in your life. And whenever you live independently of God, focusing on yourself instead of Christ, seeking material and worldly things over spiritual and eternal things, he has succeeded. The world's answer to this conflict of identity is to puff up the ego while denying God His rightful place as Lord. Satan couldn't be more pleased—that was his plan from the beginning.

Truth Encounter

Read:

Matthew 16:24-27

Reflect:

1. How is the secular worldview affecting your understanding of Satan's activity in the world?

2. Do you know people who are seriously involved in the New Age or in the occult? What effect is it having on their lives?

3. Why do you think we have so much trouble denying ourselves, picking up our cross daily, and following Jesus? What are some practical ways you can pick up your cross daily and follow Jesus?

4. What are some of the temporary pleasures Satan uses to distract us from following Christ?

Respond:

Pray and ask the Lord for insight into how you deny yourself, pick up your cross daily, and follow Him. Ask the Lord to bring to mind special ways you can sacrifice the temporary things in life to gain the eternal.

You Have Every Right to Be Free

THREE

LYDIA WAS DEALT A BAD HAND in life right from the beginning. Memories of suffering sexual abuse as a young child had haunted her continually throughout her Christian life. When she came to see me (Neil), her damaged self-image seemed beyond repair. As she told me her story, Lydia displayed little emotion, but her words reflected total despair.

"Who are you, Lydia? How do you see yourself?" I asked.

"I'm evil," she answered. "I'm just no good for anybody. People tell me I'm evil, and all I do is bring trouble."

"You're not evil," I argued. "How can a child of God be evil? Is that how you see yourself?" Lydia nodded.

I reached for a sheet of printed paper with a number of statements describing who we are in Christ* based on verses in the Bible and handed it to Lydia.

Who Am I?

Matthew 5:13	I am the salt of the earth
Matthew 5:14	I am the light of the world
John 1:12	I am a child of God

---

* Neil Anderson and Dave Park, *Stomping Out the Darkness* (Ventura, CA: Regal Books, 1993). Used by permission.

John 15:1,5	I am part of the true vine, and Christ's life flows through me
John 15:15	I am Christ's friend
John 15:16	I am chosen by Christ to bear fruit
Acts 1:8	I am Christ's personal witness sent out to tell everybody about Him
Romans 6:18	I am a slave of righteousness
Romans 6:22	I am a slave to God, making me holy and giving me eternal life
Romans 8:14,15; Galatians 3:26; 4:6	I am a child of God; I can call Him my Father
Romans 8:17	I am a co-heir with Christ, inheriting His glory
1 Corinthians 3:16; 6:19	I am a temple—a dwelling place—for God; His Spirit and His life live in me
1 Corinthians 6:17	I am joined forever to the Lord and am one spirit with Him
1 Corinthians 12:27	I am a part of Christ's body
2 Corinthians 5:17	I am a new person—my past is forgiven and everything is new
2 Corinthians 5:18,19	I am at peace with God, and He has given me the work of helping others find peace with Him
Galatians 3:26,28	I am a child of God and am one with others in His family
Galatians 4:6,7	I am a child of God and will receive the inheritance He has promised

Ephesians 1:1; Philippians 1:1;
Colossians 1:2 . . . . I am a saint, a holy person

Ephesians 2:10 . . . . I am God's handiwork, created
in Christ to do His work

Ephesians 2:19 . . . . I am a citizen of heaven along
with all of God's family

Ephesians 3:1; 4:1 . . . . I am a prisoner of Christ so I
can help others

Ephesians 4:24 . . . . I am righteous and holy

Philippians 3:20;
Ephesians 2:6 . . . . I am a citizen of heaven seated
in heaven right now

Colossians 3:3 . . . . I am hidden with Christ in God

Colossians 3:4 . . . . I am an expression of the life of
Christ because He is my life

Colossians 3:12;
1 Thessalonians 1:4 . . . . I am chosen by God, holy and
dearly loved

1 Thessalonians 5:5 . . . . I am a child of light and not of
darkness

Hebrews 3:1 . . . . I am chosen to share in God's
heavenly calling

Hebrews 3:14 . . . . I am part of Christ; I share in
His life

1 Peter 2:5 . . . . I am one of God's living stones
who are being built up in Christ
as a spiritual house

1 Peter 2:9,10 . . . . I am a member of a chosen race,
a royal priesthood, a holy nation,
a people belonging to God

1 Peter 2:11	I am only a visitor to this world, in which I temporarily live
1 Peter 5:8	I am an enemy of the devil
1 John 3:1,2	I am a child of God, and I will be like Christ when He returns
1 John 5:18	I am born again in Christ, and the evil one—the devil—cannot touch me
Exodus 3:14; John 8:24, 28,58	I am *not* the great "I am,"
1 Corinthians 15:10	but by the grace of God, I am what I am

"Would you read these statements aloud right now?" I asked. "They will remind you of what the Bible says about you, and who you are in Christ."

Lydia took the paper and began to read the first statement aloud rather haltingly. Suddenly her face changed. She looked up and sneered, "No way, you dirty son of a —!"

It is never nice to see the evil one show his ugly personality through a victim like Lydia. But I took authority over him through prayer in Christ's name and led Lydia through the Steps to Freedom in Christ. She was able to gain a new understanding of who she really is in Christ. She began to see herself as the result of what Christ did on the cross instead of being a victim of her past.

Satan had deceived Lydia into believing she was worthless and evil, which was a lie. He was dead set against her reading those statements of truth about her identity as a child of God. He knew that God's truth would uncover his lie just as surely as the light dispels the darkness. And he wasn't about to give up without a fight.

You Are a Child of God

Nothing is more basic to our freedom from Satan's bondage than understanding what God has done for us in Christ and who we are as a result. Our attitudes, actions, responses, and reactions to life's circumstances are determined by how we see ourselves. If you see yourself as the helpless victim of Satan and his schemes, you will probably live as though you were his victim and be in bondage to his lies. But if you see yourself as the dearly loved and accepted child of God that you really are, you will live like a child of God.

In this chapter, we want to highlight several critical aspects of our identity and position in Christ. Many of you have already internalized the biblical truths summarized here, but others of you may find this section to be a little on the heavy side because of its doctrinal content. But we urge you not to skip over this review on your way to the more practical chapters. These concepts are foundational to your freedom from spiritual conflict as a child of God. The issue of spiritual identity and maturity in Christ is so vital that we again suggest you work through *Stomping Out the Darkness* (published by Regal Books) together with your reading of this book. (And again, for a more in-depth theological study of positional and progressive sanctification, see the books *Radical Image* and *Higher Ground*, which we mentioned earlier.)

You Are Spiritually and Therefore Eternally Alive

Each of us is made up of two major parts: our outer self and our inner self. On the outside we have a physical body, and on the inside we have a soul/spirit. The word "soul" describes our ability to think (our mind), to feel (our emotions), and to choose (our will). The word "spirit" describes our ability to relate to God. Our body is united with our soul/spirit, and that makes us physically alive. As Christians, our soul/spirit is united with God, and that makes us spiritually alive.

When God created Adam, he was totally alive—physically and spiritually. But because of Adam's sin and spiritual death, every person who comes into the world is born physically alive but spiritually dead. Being separated from God, we lack the wisdom of God in our lives, so we learn to live independently of God, centering our interests on ourselves. Our learned independence from God is referred to in the Bible as the "flesh."

When we were born again, our soul/spirit was united with God and we came alive spiritually, as alive as Adam was in the garden before he sinned. We are now in Christ, and Christ is in us. Since Christ, who is in us, is eternal, the spiritual life we have received from Him is eternal. We don't have to wait until we die to get eternal life; we possess it right now! And contrary to what Satan would like us to believe, he can't ever take eternal life away from us—because he can't take Jesus away from us, who promised never to leave us or forsake us (Hebrews 13:5).

You Are Changed from Sinner to Saint

Have you ever heard a Christian say, "I'm just a sinner saved by grace"? Have you referred to yourself that way? If you see yourself as a sinner, you will probably sin. What would you expect a sinner to do? There will be little in your life to distinguish you from a non-Christian, and you will be filled with feelings of defeat.

Satan will seize that opportunity, pour on the guilt, and convince you that you are doomed to a roller-coaster spiritual life. As a defeated Christian, you will confess your sin and try to do better, but inwardly you will admit that you are just a sinner saved by grace, hanging on until Christ returns for you.

Is that who you really are? No way! The Bible doesn't refer to believers as sinners, not even sinners saved by grace. Believers are called saints—holy ones—who sometimes sin. We become saints at the moment of salvation—that's called justification. We live and grow as saints in our daily experience—that's called sanctification—as we continue to affirm who we really are in Christ. Seeing yourself as a saint instead of a sinner will have a powerful, positive effect on your daily ability to have victory over sin and Satan.

You Have Been Given God's Divine Nature

Ephesians 2:1-3 describes our nature *before* we came to Christ: "You were dead in your trespasses and sins, in which you formerly walked according to the course of this world, according to the prince of the power of the air...and were by nature children of wrath." Before we became Christians our very nature was sin, and the result of our sin was death (separation from God).

But at salvation God changed us. We received "the divine nature, having escaped the corruption that is in the world by lust" (2 Peter 1:4). You are no longer in the flesh; you are in Christ. You had a sinful nature because you were separated from God, but now you are a partaker of Christ's divine nature. You didn't *become* God, but you received God's divine nature.

Paul said it this way: "You were formerly darkness, but now you are Light in the Lord; walk as children of Light" (Ephesians 5:8); "Therefore if anyone is in Christ, he is a new creature" (2 Corinthians 5:17). In the face of Satan's accusations that we are no different than we were before Christ, we must believe and live in harmony with the fact that we are eternally different in Christ.

The New Testament refers to the person we were before we received Christ as our "old self." When we received Christ as Savior, our old self, which lived independently of God, died (Romans 6:6). Our new self, inspired by our new identity in Christ and committed to live in dependence on God, came to life (Galatians 2:20). Being spiritually alive means your soul is in union with God and you are identified with Him:

Romans 6:3; Galatians 2:20;
Colossians 3:1-3 . . . . In His death

Romans 6:4 . . . . In His burial

Romans 6:5,8,11 . . . . In His resurrection

Ephesians 2:6 . . . . In His ascension

Romans 5:10,11 . . . . In His life

Ephesians 1:19,20 . . . . In His power

Romans 8:16,17;
Ephesians 1:11,12 . . . . In His inheritance

Our old self had to die in order to end our relationship with sin, which controlled it. Being a new person doesn't mean that we are sinless (1 John 1:8). But since our old self has been crucified and buried with Christ, we no longer *need* to sin (1 John 2:1). We sin when we choose to act independently of God.

You Can Be Victorious over the Flesh and Sin

When our old sinful self died, sin's rule as our master ended. But sin is still around. It is strong and appealing, but its power and authority have been broken (Romans 8:2).

Also, our flesh, that part of us which was trained to live independently of God before we met Christ, did not die either. We still have memories, habits, and thought patterns in our brain which tempt us to focus on our own interests. We are no longer *in the flesh* as our old self was; we are now *in Christ*. But we can still choose to *walk according to the flesh* (Romans 8:12,13), obeying those old urges to serve ourselves instead of God.

It is our task to crucify the flesh (Romans 8:13) on a daily basis by learning to walk according to the Spirit (Galatians 5:16) and by replacing our old thought patterns with new patterns based on God's Word. That process is called "renewing our mind" (Romans 12:2).

Romans 6:11 summarizes what we are to believe about our relationship to sin because of our position in Christ: "Even so consider yourselves to be dead to sin, but alive to God in Christ Jesus." It doesn't matter whether we *feel* dead to sin or not; we are to *consider* it so because it *is* so. When we choose to believe what is true about ourselves and sin, and walk on the basis of what we believe, our right relationship with God will work out in our experience.

After teaching us what to *believe* about sin, Paul teaches us how to *relate* to sin:

> Therefore do not let sin reign in your mortal body so that you obey its lusts; and do not go on presenting the members of your body to sin as instruments of unrighteousness; but present yourselves

> to God as those alive from the dead, and your
> members as instruments of righteousness to God"
> (Romans 6:12,13).

For instance, you can't commit a sexual sin and not use your body as an instrument of unrighteousness. If you do commit a sexual sin, you will allow sin to reign (rule) *in* your mortal body. The only way that we know to help people get out of sexual bondage is to have them renounce (turn their back on) every sinful sexual use of their body and then commit it to the Lord.

We are dead to sin, but we still have the capacity to serve it by putting our bodies at sin's disposal. It's up to us to choose whether we're going to let our bodies be used for sin or for righteousness. To illustrate, suppose your youth pastor asks to use your car to deliver food baskets to the needy. Moments later a drug dealer asks to use your car to pick up one of his drug shipments. It's your car, and you can choose to lend it however you want, for good or for evil. Which would you choose? There should be no question!

Your body is yours to use to serve either God or sin and Satan, but the choice is up to you. That's why Paul wrote so insistently: "I plead with you to give your bodies to God. Let them be a living sacrifice, holy—the kind he can accept. When you think of what he has done for you, is this too much to ask?" (Romans 12:1 TLB). Because of Christ's victory over sin, you can choose not to obey sin as your master. It is your responsibility not to let sin rule in your body.

You Can Be Free from the Power of Sin

Not allowing sin to rule my body sounds wonderful, Neil and Dave, you may be thinking. *But you don't know how hard*

*my battle with sin is. I find myself doing what I shouldn't do
and not doing what I should do. It's a constant struggle.*

Yes, we know how hard the battle with sin is. So did the
apostle Paul. He wrote Romans 7:15-25 out of the same feelings of frustration that you may be experiencing. In this passage, we discover God's path to freedom from the power of
sin.

I (Neil) invite you to listen in as I walk through these
verses with Dan, who is struggling to overcome the power of
sin in his life:

Neil: Dan, let's look at this verse that seems to describe what
          you are now experiencing. Romans 7:15 reads: "I don't
          understand myself at all, for I really want to do what is
          right, but I can't. I do what I don't want to—what I
          hate" (TLB). Would you say that this verse describes you?

Dan: Exactly! I want to do what God says is right, but some-
          times I find myself doing just the opposite.

Neil: You probably identify with verse 16 as well: "But if I do
          the very thing I do not want to do, I agree with the Law,
          confessing that the Law is good." Dan, how many per-
          sonalities or players are mentioned in this verse?

Dan: There is only one person, and it is clearly "I."

Neil: It's very defeating when we know what we want to do,
          but for some reason can't do it. How have you tried to
          figure this out in your own mind?

Dan: Sometimes I wonder if I'm even a Christian. It seems to
          work for others, but not for me. Often I wonder if the
          Christian life is even possible or if God is really here.

Neil: If you and God were the only players in this scenario, it would be reasonable to blame either God or yourself for your predicament. But now look at verse 17: "So now, no longer am I the one doing it, but sin which dwells in me." How many players are there now, Dan?

Dan: Two, I guess, but I don't understand.

Neil: Let's read verse 18 and see if we can make some sense out of it: "For I know that nothing good dwells in me, that is, in my flesh."

Dan: I learned that verse a long time ago. It's been easy to accept the fact that I'm no good.

Neil: That's not what it says, Dan. In fact, it says just the opposite. *Whatever it is that is dwelling in you* is not *you*. If I had a wood splinter in my finger, it would be "nothing good" dwelling in me. But the "nothing good" isn't me; it's the splinter. It's also important to note that this "nothing good" is not even my flesh, but it's dwelling *in* my flesh. If we saw only ourselves in this struggle, we wouldn't stand a chance to live righteously. But there's something else involved in our struggle with sin, and its nature is different from ours.

You see, Dan, when you and I were born, we were born under the *penalty* of sin. And we know that Satan and his demons are always working to keep us under that penalty. When God saved us, Satan lost that battle, but he didn't curl up his tail or pull in his fangs. He is now committed to keep us under the *power* of sin. He's going to work through our flesh, that old pattern of living independently of God that remains after salvation.

Let's read on to see if we can learn more about how this battle is being fought: "For the good that I want, I do not do; but I practice the very evil that I do not want. But if I am doing the very thing I do not want, I am no longer the one doing it, but sin which dwells in me. I find then the principle that evil is present in me, the one who wants to do good" (verses 19-21).

Can you figure out from these passages what the nature is of that "nothing good" that dwells in you?

Dan: Sure, it's clearly evil and sin. But isn't it just my own sin? When I sin I feel so guilty.

Neil: There is no question that you and I sin, but we are not "sin." Evil is present in us, but we are not "evil" itself. This does not excuse us for sinning, however, because Paul wrote earlier that it is our responsibility not to let sin rule in our bodies (Romans 6:12). Do you ever feel so defeated that you just want to strike out at someone or yourself?

Dan: Almost every day!

Neil: But when you cool down, do you again start thinking in a way that's in line with who you are in Christ?

Dan: Always, and then I feel awful about lashing out.

Neil: Verse 22 explains this cycle: "In my inner being I delight in God's law"(NIV). When we act out of character with who we really are, the Holy Spirit immediately brings conviction because of our relationship with God, and we often take it out on ourselves. But soon our true nature expresses itself again, and we are drawn back to God.

It's like the frustrated teenager who announces that he's running away from home. He wants out and couldn't care less about how Mom and Dad feel. But after he gets in touch with his pain and expresses his emotions, he softens and says, "I really do love my parents, and I don't want to run away. But I just don't see any other way out." That's his inner person, his true self, talking.

Verse 23 describes the nature of this battle with sin: "But I see a different law in the members of my body, waging war against the law of my mind and making me a prisoner of the law of sin which is in my members." According to this verse, Dan, where is the battle being fought?

Dan: The battle looks like it's in the mind.

Neil: That's precisely where the battle rages. Now if Satan can get you to think you are the only one in the battle, you will get down on either yourself or God when you sin. Let me put it this way: Suppose there is a talking dog on the other side of a closed door and the dog is saying, "Come on, let me in. You know you want to. Everybody's doing it. You'll get away with it. After all, who's going to know?" So you open the door, and the dog comes in and clamps his teeth around your leg. On the other side of the door, the dog plays the role of the tempter, but once you let the dog in, he plays the role of the accuser. "You opened the door! You opened the door!" And what do you do?

Dan: I usually end up confessing because I feel so guilty. But in my struggle with sin, nobody's ever told me about this tempting and accusing dog! I usually end up beating on myself, but now I think I should beat on the dog.

Neil: I find that people eventually get tired of beating on themselves, so they walk away from God under a cloud of defeat and condemnation. On the other hand, just beating on the dog is not enough either. You did the right thing to confess to God, which means you agreed with Him that you did open the door, but that's not enough. Confession is only the first step in repentance. Christians who only do that get stuck in the sin-confess-sin-confess-sin-confess cycle and eventually give up. You submitted to God when you agreed with Him that you opened the door; now you need to resist the devil, and he will flee from you (James 4:7). Finally, go back and slam the door shut, and don't get suckered into opening it again. Repentance isn't complete until you've truly changed.

Paul expressed this feeling of unresolved conflict in verse 24: "Wretched man that I am! Who will set me free from the body of this death?" He's not saying *"wicked* or *sinful* man that I am"; he's saying, *"miserable* man that I am." There's nobody more miserable than the person who knows what's right and wants to do what's right, but for some reason can't. He's defeated because he's in bondage. His attempts to do the right thing are met with defeat. He wonders, *Is there any victory?*

The answer starts to come in verse 25: "Thanks be to God through Jesus Christ our Lord! So then, on the one hand I myself with my mind am serving the law of God, but on the other, with my flesh the law of sin."

Now let's read Romans chapter 8 and see how Paul overcomes the law of sin by the law of life in Christ Jesus.

Dan: I think I'm getting it. I've been feeling guilty because I can't live the Christian life—but I haven't really understood *how* to live it. I've tried to overcome this sin by myself, and I haven't really understood the battle for my mind.

Neil: You're on the right track. Beating yourself up and condemning yourself won't help because there is no condemnation for those who are in Christ Jesus (Romans 8:1,2). Let's see if we can resolve your conflict with genuine repentance and faith in God. I'd like to walk you through these Steps to Freedom. Then we can talk about how to win that battle for your mind and learn how to walk by faith in the power of the Holy Spirit. Then you won't carry out the desires of your flesh (Galatians 5:16).

Truth Encounter

Read:

Romans 7:15-25

Reflect:

1. How will seeing yourself as a saint instead of a sinner have a powerful and positive effect on your daily victory over sin and Satan?

2. In what ways were we trained to live independently of God before we met Christ? How do we overcome those old urges to serve ourselves, and learn how to serve God?

3. What did you learn most from the conversation between Neil and Dan?

4. Repeated acts form habits. How are bad habits or strongholds destroyed?

Respond:

Pray and ask the Lord to reveal to your mind any strongholds or bad habits that you might have. Turn to the "Who Am I?" list on pages 45–48, and read through it out loud and carefully.

You Can Win the Battle for Your Mind

FOUR

HE RESCUED US FROM THE domain of darkness, and transferred us to the kingdom of His beloved Son, in whom we have redemption, the forgiveness of sins" (Colossians 1:13,14). "If anyone is in Christ, he is a new creature; the old things passed away; behold, new things have come" (2 Corinthians 5:17). "You have died and your life is hidden with Christ in God" (Colossians 3:3).

"If those verses are true, then how come I still struggle with the same thoughts and feelings I did before I became a Christian?" We suspect that every honest Christian has asked that question or at least thought about it. There is a very logical reason why you still think, feel, and too often act as you did before you were born again.

When you were just a little squirt, during the formative years of your life, you had neither the presence of God in your life nor the knowledge of His ways. So you learned to live your life without depending on God. This learned independence from God is a major characteristic of what the Bible calls the "flesh."

When you became a new creation in Christ, nobody pushed the delete button in your memory bank. Everything you learned before Christ (and all the feelings that go with it) is still recorded in your memory. That is why Paul said, "Do not conform any longer to the pattern of this world, but be transformed by the renewing of your mind" (Romans 12:2 NIV). Even as believers we can still be conformed to this world by listening to the wrong programs, visiting the wrong websites, or reading the wrong things.

Strongholds of Self-Defense

In our natural state before Christ, we learned a lot of ways to cope with life or defend ourselves that weren't healthy. Psychologists call these unhealthy patterns of living "defense mechanisms," and they certainly don't mix with Christianity. For instance, many people have learned to lie in order to protect themselves. Other common defense mechanisms include:

- denial (conscious or subconscious refusal to face the truth)
- fantasy (escaping from the real world)
- emotional insulation (withdrawing to avoid rejection)
- regression (reverting to less threatening times)
- displacement (taking out frustrations on others)
- projection (blaming others)
- rationalization (making excuses for poor behavior)

Defense mechanisms are like what Paul calls "strongholds." He writes, "Though we walk in the flesh, we do not war according to the flesh, for the weapons of our warfare are not of the flesh, but divinely powerful for the destruction of fortresses. We are destroying speculations and every lofty thing raised up against the knowledge of God, and we are taking every thought captive to the obedience of Christ" (2 Corinthians 10:3-5).

"Fortresses" (or strongholds) are fleshly patterns of thinking that were programmed into your mind when you learned to live your life independently of God. Your world-view was shaped by the environment you grew up in. But when you became a Christian, nobody pressed the "CLEAR" button. Your old fleshly thinking patterns weren't erased.

What you learned has to be unlearned. If you have been trained wrong, can you be retrained? If you have believed a lie, can you renounce that lie and choose to believe the truth? Can your mind be reprogrammed? That is what repentance is: a change of mind.

We are transformed by the renewing of our minds. We can be transformed because we have the mind of Christ within us and because the Holy Spirit will lead us into all truth. But the world system we grew up in and our own fleshly thinking patterns are not the only enemies of our becoming like Christ. Even though we are new creations in Him, we still battle the world, the flesh—and the devil.

When Morgan, a young Christian girl, came to see me (Dave), she was in bondage to a self-destructive eating disorder. Morgan was the only Christian in her family, and she struggled with insecurity and feelings of being unloved. She was caught in a vicious cycle of overeat-vomit-confess-overeat-vomit-confess. Day after day she lived this nightmare.

My wife, Grace, and I met with her for six hours one day, leading her through the Steps to Freedom in Christ. When she left she was a different girl. She no longer needed to beat on herself for the sin and evil that prompted her sick behavior.

Shortly after our meeting with Morgan we received the following letter:

> Dear Dave and Grace,
>
> I found myself overeating late this afternoon. Why? Because I was tired. When I'm tired I pressure myself over the edge to do more work, so I overeat. I prayed for God's forgiveness. Thoughts that I should throw up raced into my mind. I was alone. I could have done it. But God would not be glorified if I did that.
>
> Here are the thoughts I allowed into my mind: 1) I'm tired. 2) Satan, you are a rotten liar. 3) God, my body is Your temple. 4) I have been bought with a price; I'm not my own. 5) I could be glorifying God in some other way, not vomiting to make myself feel better. 6) I have people in my life who love me. 7) I don't have to punish myself anymore. 8) I am not bad; in fact, I am righteous. 9) As a precious child of God I will not harm my body or my spirit or my mind with the destruction I cause in my body when I throw up.
>
> I'm laughing now. It feels so good to be in control of myself. This is freedom in Christ.
>
> Love in Christ,
>
> —Morgan

We hope you're sensing the fact that victory is truly available for those who are in Christ. There is a war raging, but we are on the winning side, for we are more than conquerors in Christ!

Satan's Schemes

Even though you're on the winning side, don't think that Satan is no longer interested in manipulating your mind in order to achieve his purposes. Satan's constant aim is to get his thoughts in your head and to promote his lie in the face of God's truth. He knows that if he can control your thoughts, he can control your life. And if he can control your life, you will not experience the victory that Christ has won for you. That is why Paul said, "We are taking every thought captive to the obedience of Christ" (2 Corinthians 10:5). In this verse the word "thought" is the Greek word *noema*. To understand this passage, we've found it helpful to see how Paul uses this word elsewhere in this second letter to the Corinthian church.

Paul tells the church to forgive after the believers carry out church discipline. "One whom you forgive anything, I forgive also; for indeed what I have forgiven, if I have forgiven anything, I did it for your sakes in the presence of Christ, so that no advantage would be taken of us by Satan, for we are not ignorant of his schemes *[noema]*" (2 Corinthians 2:10,11). The word "schemes" comes from that same root word, *noema*. Satan really takes advantage of those won't forgive. After helping thousands of students find their freedom in Christ, we can testify that unforgiveness is the major reason young people remain in bondage to the past.

Concerning evangelism, Paul wrote, "If our gospel is veiled, it is veiled to those who are perishing, in whose case the god of this world has blinded the minds *[noema]* of the unbelieving so that they might not see the light of the gospel of the glory of Christ, who is the image of God" (2 Corinthians 4:3,4). How are we going to reach this world for Christ if Satan has blinded the minds of unbelievers? The answer is prayer.

Paul also wrote, "I am afraid that, as the serpent deceived Eve by his craftiness, your minds *[noema]* will be led astray from the simplicity and purity of devotion to Christ" (2 Corinthians 11:3).

A student named Jay had an experience that really shows how deceptive thoughts from Satan can be. Jay came into my office one day and said, "Dr. Anderson, I'm in trouble."

"What's the problem, Jay?"

"When I sit down to study I get prickly sensations all over my body, my vision gets blurry, and I can't concentrate."

"Tell me about your walk with God," I probed.

"I have a very close walk with God," Jay boasted.

"What do you mean?"

"Well, when I leave school at noon each day, I ask God where He wants me to go for lunch. If I hear a thought that says, 'Burger King,' I go to Burger King. Then I ask Him what He wants me to eat. If the thought comes to order a Whopper, I order a Whopper."

"What about your church attendance?" I continued.

"I go every Sunday wherever God tells me to go. And for the last three Sundays God has told me to go to a Mormon church."

I immediately knew that Satan was invading Jay's thoughts because God would never send a Christian to a church with a twisted doctrine of Christ and God's Word.

Jay sincerely wanted to do what God wanted him to do. But he was listening to his thoughts as if they were God's voice instead of "taking every thought captive to the obedience of Christ" (2 Corinthians 10:5). He had opened himself up to Satan's schemes in his life. Satan is clever. He doesn't rumble in like a bull in a china shop; he slithers in like a snake in the grass (2 Corinthians 11:3).

Satan and Our Minds

Scripture clearly teaches that Satan can put thoughts into our minds. In the Old Testament, "Satan rose up against Israel and incited David to take a census of Israel" (1 Chronicles 21:1 NIV). What's wrong with taking a census? Shouldn't David know how many troops he has to take into combat?

But this really shows the sneaky nature of Satan. He knew that David had a whole heart for God and wouldn't willingly defy the Lord. The strategy Satan chose was to get David to put his confidence in his own resources rather than in God's resources. This was the same David who wrote, "A horse is a false hope for victory" (Psalm 33:17). David knew the battle belonged to the Lord, but suddenly he had this "thought" to take a census (against the protests of his general Joab, who knew it was sin). Tragically, 70,000 men of Israel died as the result of David's sin.

How did Satan incite David? Did he talk audibly to David? No, these thoughts were David's thoughts. At least he believed they were. There's where Satan's trick is. These lying thoughts come "first person singular" ("*I* want to..."; "*I* will do that") so that we think they're our own thoughts. The battle for your mind involves more than just "self-talk."

Judas also listened to the devil. "During supper, the devil having already put into the heart of Judas Iscariot, the son of Simon, to betray Him" (John 13:2). We may want to think that Judas' act was just a bad decision prompted by the flesh, but Scripture clearly says that Judas' thoughts came from Satan. And when Judas realized what he had done, he took his own life. "The thief comes only to steal and kill and destroy" (John 10:10). Death also resulted in the early church when Satan filled the heart of Ananias to lie to the Holy Spirit (Acts 5:3).

"Not Against Flesh and Blood"

We have counseled hundreds of young believers who are weighed down by their thought life. Some have difficulty concentrating and reading their Bible, while others actually hear "voices" or struggle with accusing and condemning thoughts. In fact, the surveys that Freedom in Christ Ministries has made over the years have continued to show that about 70 percent of the born-again students we come in contact with either claim to hear voices or struggle with accusing and condemning thoughts.

With few exceptions, these struggles have turned out to be a spiritual battle for their minds. This shouldn't surprise us, since we have been warned in 1 Timothy 4:1 (NIV): "The Spirit clearly says that in later times some will abandon the faith and follow deceiving spirits and things taught by demons."

Why don't we as believers in Christ wake up and pay attention to this? For one thing, we can't read your mind, and you can't read our minds. So none of us really has any idea what's going on in the minds of other people unless they have the courage to share with us. In many cases they won't, because in our society many people will assume they're a mental case.

So they'll tell you about their negative *experiences;* but only with the right person will they dare share what is going on *inside*. Are they crazy, or is there a battle going on for their mind? If we're "ignorant of Satan's schemes," we can only come to the conclusion, "Any problem in the mind must either be a chemical imbalance or a pattern of the flesh."

Psychologists and psychiatrists routinely see patients who are hearing voices; "chemical imbalance" is their standard diagnosis. We believe that our body chemistry can get out of balance and cause discomfort and that hormonal problems can throw our systems off. But we also believe that other valid questions need to be asked, such as, "How can a chemical produce a personal thought?" and "How can our neurotransmitters involuntarily and randomly fire in such a way that they create thoughts that we are opposed to thinking?" Is there a natural explanation? We have to remain open to any legitimate answers and explanations, but we will probably not have a complete answer unless we also take into account the reality of the spiritual world.

When students say they are hearing voices, what are they actually hearing? The only way we can *physically* hear is to have a sound source. Sound waves move from the source through the medium of air and strike our eardrums, which send a signal to our brains. That is how we physically hear. But the "voices" that young people hear or the "thoughts" that they struggle with are not coming from a physical source if others around them are not hearing what they hear.

In the same way, when people say they see things (that others don't), what are they actually seeing? The only way that we can naturally see something is to have a light source reflecting from a material object to our eyes, which then send a signal to our brain. Satan and his demons are spiritual beings. They don't have material substance, so we can't see them or any spiritual being with our natural eyes or hear them with our ears. "Our struggle is not against *flesh and blood*, but against the rulers, against the authorities, against the powers of this dark world and against the spiritual forces of evil in the heavenly realms" (Ephesians 6:12 NIV, emphasis added).

Brain vs. Mind

There is much we don't know about how we function mentally, but we do know that there's a big difference between our brains and our minds. Our brains are organic matter. When we die physically, we're separated from our bodies, and our brain turns back into dust. At that moment we'll be absent from our bodies and present with the Lord. But we won't be mindless, because the mind is a part of the soul.

Here's an analogy. Our ability to think is like the way a computer functions. Both involve two separate components: One is the hardware, which is the actual physical computer (the brain); the other is the software, which programs the hardware (the mind). Since the software is nonphysical, if it is removed from the hardware, the hardware still weighs the same. Likewise, if the spirit is removed from the body, the body also remains the same weight. A computer is totally worthless without the software, but the software won't work either if the hardware shuts down.

Our society assumes that if something is not functioning right between your ears it must be a hardware problem. On the contrary, we don't believe the main problem is with the hardware; we think the main problem is in the software. Romans 12:1,2 says we are to submit our bodies to God (which includes our brain) and be transformed by the renewing of our minds.

After hearing a talk that I (Neil) gave about this, one woman wanted some clarification. She said, "I recently visited my daughter on the mission field, and I contracted malaria. I got so sick that I almost died. At the height of my fever, I started to hallucinate. Are you telling me that those hallucinations were demonic?"

"What were you hallucinating about?" I asked.

"Mostly about Pluto, Mickey Mouse, Donald Duck, and Daisy," she replied.

I couldn't help but chuckle. "Did you stop at Disneyland on your way to the mission field?" I inquired.

She responded, "Well yes, I did. How did you know?"

There was certainly nothing demonic about her experience. Her visit to Disneyland was fresh on her mind. When you go to sleep or slip into a coma, your physical brain continues to function, but there are "no hands on the keyboard." If you are mentally active and pounding away on the keyboard of your mind, you are not asleep. You go to sleep when you stop thinking. But while you are sleeping, your brain will continue to work away and will randomly access whatever has been stored in your memory.

To illustrate, consider the content of your dreams. Don't they almost always relate to people you know, things you have seen, or places you have been? The stories in your dreams can be pretty creative, but the people and places have already been programmed into your memory. For instance, suppose a child watches a horror movie, then goes to sleep and has a nightmare. Chances are the players in the nightmare will be the same ones as in the movie.

But when someone has grotesque nightmares that cannot be traced to something previously seen or heard, then we would say that the dream is demonic. When we take students through the Steps to Freedom in Christ, that kind of nightmare stops.

The Battle Is Real

This spiritual battle for our minds needs to be exposed for what it is, so that we can really help people who experience it. Here's an illustration why. What typically happens when frightened children come into their parents' bedroom and say they saw or heard something in their room? One of the parents would probably go into the child's room, look in the closet or under the bed, and say, "There's nothing in your room, honey—now go back to sleep!"

If you are a young person or an adult, and you saw something in *your* room, would *you* just forget about it and go back to sleep? "But I looked in the room. There was nothing there," the parent responds. And he or she would be correct. There never was anything in the room that could be detected by our natural senses. "Then it's not real," says the skeptic. Oh yes, it is! What that child saw or heard was in his or her *mind*, and it was *very real*.

The spiritual battle for our minds does not operate according to laws of nature we can observe. There are no physical barriers that can stop or keep out the movements of Satan. The frightened face of a child shows that the battle is real. Why not respond to a child like this?

"Honey, I believe you saw or heard something. I didn't hear or see anything, so that helps me understand. You may be under a spiritual attack, or you could be having bad memories of a movie you saw. Sometimes *I* can't tell the difference between what is real and a dream I just had.

"Before I pray for your protection, I want you to know that Jesus is much bigger and more powerful than anything you see or hear that frightens you. The Bible teaches us that Jesus, who is living in us, is greater than any monsters in the world. Because Jesus is always with us, we can tell whatever it is that is frightening us to leave in Jesus' name. The Bible tells us to submit to God and resist the devil, and he will flee from us. Can you do that, honey? Do you have any questions? Then let's pray together."

Much of what today is falsely called mental illness is nothing more than a battle for our minds. Proverbs 23:7 says, "As he thinks within himself, so he is." In other words, you don't do anything without first thinking it. Our behavior is the outcome of what we choose to think or believe. We can't see what people think. We can only observe what they do. Trying to change our behavior—without changing what we believe and therefore think—will never produce any lasting results.

Since we can't read another person's mind, we have to learn to ask the right questions. Five-year-old Danny was sent to the office of his Christian school for hurting several other children on the playground. He had been acting aggressively toward others and was restless in class. His teacher said, "I'm puzzled by his recent behavior—it isn't like Danny to act this way!" Danny's mother was also a teacher at the school. When she asked her son about Jesus, he covered his ears and shouted, "I hate Jesus!" Then he grabbed her and laughed in a hideous voice!

We asked Danny whether he ever heard voices talking to him in his head. He looked relieved at the question and volunteered that voices were shouting at him on the playground to hurt other kids. The thoughts were so loud that the only way to make them be quiet was to obey, even though he knew he would get into trouble. We told Danny that he didn't have to listen to the voices anymore. We then led him through the children's version of the Steps to Freedom having him pray the prayers after us. When we were done, we asked him how he felt. A big smile came onto his face, and with a sigh of relief he said, "Much better!" His teacher noticed new calmness in him the next day—as though he were a different child. He has not since repeated his aggressive behavior in school.

A Christian couple adopted a young boy and received him into their home with open arms. Their innocent little baby turned into a monster before he was five. Their home was in turmoil when I (Neil) was asked to talk to him. After some friendly chatting, I asked him if it ever seemed like someone was talking to him in his head.

"Yes," he said, "all the time."

"What are they saying?"

"They're telling me that I'm no good."

I then asked him whether he'd ever invited Jesus into his life. He replied, "Yes, but I didn't mean it."

I told him if he really did ask Jesus to come into his life, he could tell those voices to leave him. When he realized this, he gave his heart to Christ.

Another husband and wife heard thumping on the wall of their son's room. He had apparently taken a pair of scissors and stabbed the wall several times. They never caught him doing it, nor did they find the scissors. Then their boy began to cut up every piece of clothing in the house. Again they never actually caught their son doing it. Huge medical and counseling bills piled up as they desperately tried to find a solution. Finally the parents were introduced to our material and began to think that this might possibly be a spiritual problem. So they asked their son whether he ever had thoughts telling him to do what he was doing. He said, "Yes, and if I didn't do what they told me to do, they said they would kill you [the father]!" The little boy thought he was saving his father's life!

The spiritual battle for your mind is graphically illustrated in this letter we received:

I wanted to thank you for showing me how to be free of something I always suspected was spiritual, but I was never quite sure about it. For years, ever since I was a teenager (I am now 36), I had these "voices" in my head. There were four in particular, and sometimes what seemed like loud choruses of them. When the subject of schizophrenia would come up on television or in a magazine I would think to myself, *I know I am not schizophrenic, but what is this in my head???*

I was tortured, mocked, and jeered. Every single thought I had was second-guessed, and consequently I had zero self-esteem. I often wished the voices would be quiet, and I always wondered if other people heard voices as well and if it was "common."

When I started to learn from you about taking every thought captive to the obedience of Christ, and when I read about other people's experiences with these voices, I came to recognize them for what they were, and I was able to make them leave.

This was an amazing and beautiful thing—to be fully quiet in my mind, after so many years of torment. I do not need to explain further all the wonderful things that come with this freedom of the mind—it is a blessing you seem to know well.

Taking Every Thought Captive

How do we know whether these negative, lying, and condemning thoughts are from the evil one or are just our own fleshly thinking patterns? In one sense it doesn't make any difference. We are to take *every* thought captive to the obedience of Christ; that is, if it isn't true, don't believe it. But you'll know that thoughts like this didn't come from you if you work through the Steps to Freedom and then those thoughts are no longer there. Fleshly patterns of thinking don't just leave. They are slowly replaced or overcome as we renew our minds.

Paul says we're not to be anxious (double-minded) about anything. Instead we are to turn to God in prayer, "and the peace of God, which surpasses all comprehension, will guard your hearts and your minds *[noema]* in Christ Jesus" (Philippians 4:7). The next verse says we are to let our minds dwell on those things which are true, pure, lovely, and right.

Our relationship with God is personal, and as in any relationship there are certain issues that have to be resolved in order for the relationship to work. We can't expect God to bless us if we are living in open rebellion against Him. "Rebellion is like the sin of divination, and arrogance like the evil of idolatry" (1 Samuel 15:23 NIV). If we are proud, God is opposed to us (James 4:6). If we are bitter and unwilling to forgive, God will turn us over to the torturers (Matthew 18:34). If one of these issues is interfering with your relationship with God, get it settled! Only He can help you with the battle for your mind, because He is the one who binds up the brokenhearted and sets the captive free.

Truth Encounter

Read:
2 Corinthians 10:3-5

Reflect:

1. Before Christ was a part of our lives, we learned many ways to cope with life or defend ourselves that were not healthy. Can you write down the seven different defense mechanisms we covered in this chapter?

2. In what ways have you personally relied on some of those defense mechanisms? Have any of them become strongholds in your life?

3. Can Satan or his demons put thoughts in our minds? (Check out 1 Chronicles 21:1).

4. What do we mean when we say "the battle with spiritual forces is in our minds?"

Respond:
Pray and ask the Lord to reveal to your mind any old defense mechanisms that you have been depending on. Renounce them carefully and declare today that Jesus is your strength and your only defense.

Confronting the Rebel Prince

ONE OF THE FIRST PERSONS I (Neil) dealt with about spiritual conflicts and demonic influences was Mary. She was a Christian with severe mental and emotional problems that had developed after her father divorced her mother. Within a period of five years, Mary had been admitted to a mental hospital three times. After about three weeks of counseling with me, she finally found the nerve to bring up the snakes in her life.

"What about the snakes?" I asked.

"Well, they crawl on me at night when I'm in bed," she confessed.

"What do you do when the snakes come?"

"I run in to my mother. But they always come back when I'm alone."

"I'll tell you what you should do," I continued. "When you're in bed and the snakes come, say out loud, 'In the name of Christ I command you to leave me.' "

"I couldn't do that," Mary protested. "I'm not mature enough or strong enough."

"It's not a matter of your maturity; it's a matter of your position in Christ. You have as much right to resist Satan and make him leave as I do."

Mary squirmed at the prospect. "Well, I guess I could do that," she sighed, sounding like she had just agreed to take castor oil.

The next week when Mary walked in, she said, "The snakes are gone!"

"Great! Why didn't you tell me about them sooner?"

"Because I was afraid you would get them too. Now I realize that this was just another part of Satan's lie."

Within a few months Mary was free of the devil's trap and was helping in our children's department at church.

Before we talk about the reality and present activity of Satan and his demons, you need to understand your position of authority in Christ over the powers of darkness. James wrote: "Resist the devil and he will flee from you" (James 4:7). But if you don't resist him, he doesn't have to go. Or if you just pull the covers over your head in fear and say, "O God, do something about these demonic influences," the evil spirits don't have to leave. Resisting the devil in your life is your responsibility based on the authority you possess in Christ.

Carrying Jesus' Badge of Authority

When Jesus equipped His disciples for ministry, "He called the twelve together, and gave them power and authority over all the demons and to heal diseases. And He sent them out to proclaim the kingdom of God, and to perform healing" (Luke 9:1,2). Jesus knew that when His disciples began preaching and healing the sick, demonic powers would try to stop them. So He gave them power and authority over demons.

Later Jesus sent out 70 of His followers on a similar mission, and they "returned with joy, saying, 'Lord, even the demons are subject to us in Your name' " (Luke 10:17). They were astonished at the victory they experienced over evil spirits.

But Jesus quickly reminded them that there was something even more important than their authority over evil powers: "I have given you authority over all the power of the Enemy....However, the important thing is not that demons obey you, but that your names are registered as citizens in heaven" (Luke 10:19,20 TLB). Jesus was saying, "Don't be demon-centered; be God-centered."

That's a good warning for us. As we learn to use our authority over the kingdom of darkness, we may be tempted to spend all our time studying about Satanism, the occult, and the New Age movement and looking for demons behind every door. But it's the *truth* that sets us free, not how much we know about the lies of Satan. We would have no authority at all if it weren't for our identity as children of God and our position in Christ. *Who we are* is always more important than *what we do*.

The Right and the Ability

Jesus gave His disciples both *authority* and *power* over demons. What's the difference? Authority is the *right* to rule. For example, a policeman has the right to stop traffic at an intersection because of the position of authority represented by his badge. In the same way, Jesus gave His disciples His badge to carry. They had the right to rule over the demons because of their position as followers of the One to whom all authority in heaven and on earth has been given (Matthew 28:18).

Power is the *ability* to rule. A policeman has the authority to stop traffic, but he doesn't have the physical ability to do so. If he tries to stop traffic by his own power, he will probably get run over. However, if you move a 20-foot-square cement block into the middle of the intersection, it may not have any authority to make cars stop, but it certainly has the ability to do the job!

Jesus gave His followers the *responsibility* of proclaiming the good news, and He also gave them the tools they needed to do the job. If Jesus had not given them both *authority* and *power* in the spirit world, the demons would have just laughed at their feeble attempts and sent them running for cover.

You may think, as Mary did, that you're not mature enough to resist demons who try to interfere in your life. You say, "After all, I'm just a teenager. The devil is more powerful than I am."

By yourself you don't have the ability to resist Satan and his demons. But *in Christ you do*. In the story of David and Goliath, the Israelites looked at the giant fearfully and said, "We can't fight him." But young David, probably just a teenager, looked at Goliath and said, "Who is this…Philistine, that he should taunt the armies of the living God?" (1 Samuel 17:26). Then David blew him away with his slingshot.

The army saw Goliath in relation to themselves and trembled; David saw Goliath in relation to God and triumphed. When you encounter the spiritual enemies of your soul, remember: You plus Jesus equals a majority. A little child, an aged grandmother, or a teenager in Christ have the same authority in the spiritual world as an experienced pastor. We are to "glory in Christ Jesus and put no confidence in the flesh" (Philippians 3:3).

Pulling Rank

It was an eye-opening experience for the disciples to discover that "the demons are subject to us in Your name" (Luke

10:17). This verse pictures a group of soldiers snapping to attention and precisely following the orders of their commanding officer. Jesus was telling us that the demons are the soldiers and, in Christ, we are the generals. They must do what we command in Christ's name.

We sometimes mistakenly see God and His kingdom on one side and Satan and his kingdom on the other side. Both kingdoms seem to be very powerful, and here we are, stuck in the middle between the two, like the rope in a tug-of-war. On some days God seems to be winning, and on other days the devil appears to have the upper hand. And we don't seem to have anything to say about who wins the battle.

But that's not how it is. Spiritual authority is not a tug-of-war; it's a chain of command. Jesus Christ has all authority in heaven and on earth (Matthew 28:18). He's at the top. He has given His authority and power to His children to be used in His name (Luke 10:17); we're underneath Him. What about Satan and his demons? They're at the bottom, subject to the authority Christ has given to us. They have no more right to rule our lives than a private in the army has to order a general to clean the latrine.

So why does the kingdom of darkness exercise such a powerful evil influence in the world and in the lives of so many young Christians? Because the devil is an excellent liar. Satan's power is not equal with God's; Satan has been totally defeated. But if he can deceive you into believing that he has more power and authority than you do, you will live as if he does! You have been given authority over the kingdom of darkness, but if you don't believe it and use it, it's as if you don't have it.

Jesus' Badge of Authority in Today's World

Christians today enjoy the same claim to Christ's authority in the spiritual world as the disciples who were personally sent out by Him. In fact, because of the death, resurrection, and ascension of Christ and the outpouring of the Holy Spirit, we have an even greater advantage in spiritual warfare than the first disciples did. They were *with* Christ (Mark 3:14,15), but we are *in* Christ.

That was Paul's great news in the opening lines of Ephesians. Notice how many times he mentions our position in Christ (emphasis added):

> Blessed be the God and Father of our Lord Jesus Christ, who has blessed us with every spiritual blessing in the heavenly places *in Christ,* just as He chose us *in Him* before the foundation of the world (verses 3,4)....To the praise of the glory of His grace, which He freely bestowed on us *in the Beloved. In Him* we have redemption through His blood (verses 6,7)....*In Him* also we have obtained an inheritance...to the end that we who were the first to hope *in Christ* would be to the praise of His glory. *In Him,* you also...were sealed *in Him* with the Holy Spirit of promise (verses 10-13).

Paul wanted to make sure that nobody missed his point. Everything we have is because of our personal relationship with Christ and His indwelling Spirit.

Having firmly established the reality of our position in Christ, Paul expressed his heart's desire for Spirit-controlled believers in this prayer:

> I pray that the eyes of your heart may be enlightened, so that you will know what is the hope of His calling, what are the riches of the glory of His

> inheritance in the saints, and what is the sur-
> passing greatness of His power toward us who
> believe. These are in accordance with the working
> of the strength of His might which He brought
> about in Christ, when He raised Him from the
> dead and seated Him at His right hand in heav-
> enly places (Ephesians 1:18-20).

We need to have our inner eyes opened because our problem is not that we aren't in Christ; it's that we don't *see* it or *understand* it. And when we don't understand who we are, we don't experience the freedom and fruitfulness that goes along with our position in Christ.

Paul also suggests that our problem with authority in the spiritual world is not that we aren't tapped into the surpassing greatness of Christ's power; it's that we just don't see it. And as long as we fail to see that Christ's authority is available to us, we will fail to exercise that authority in our lives, and we will live in bondage.

The reason Christ gave us His authority was to demonstrate to the kingdom of darkness who really is in control in this world. In Ephesians 3:8-10, Paul wrote: "To me, the very least of all saints, this grace was given, to preach to the Gentiles the unfathomable riches of Christ...so that the manifold wisdom of God might now be made known through the church to the rulers and the authorities in the heavenly places." "Heavenly places" is not a physical place; it is a spiritual realm.

How are we doing at making Christ's victory known to "the rulers and the authorities in heavenly places"? In most youth groups, not very well. Some of us are still saying, "What rulers and authorities?" We're not sure that demons even exist. How are we ever going to get our job done in the world if we don't believe what God says about the kingdom of darkness?

Others of us are hiding in a corner pleading, "O God, please help us! The devil is roaring at us!" And God responds, "I've done all I'm going to do. I defeated and disarmed Satan at the cross. I gave you all the authority you need in Christ. Now open your eyes. Realize who you are and assume your responsibility with the authority you already have."

Do You Have What It Takes?

How do we appropriate Christ's authority over spiritual powers? Does every Christian have this authority regardless of age or level of spiritual maturity? Yes, every believer has spiritual authority because of his or her position in Christ. But there are four qualifications for exercising authority over rulers and authorities in the spiritual world.

1. *Belief.* Imagine a rookie traffic cop approaching a busy intersection to direct traffic for the first time. They told him at the academy that all he had to do was step into the street and hold up his hand and the cars would stop, but he's not so sure. He stands on the curb, tweets his whistle weakly, and sort of waves at an oncoming car, which just roars by him. His authority is limited by his lack of confidence.

Now imagine a veteran officer coming on the scene. He sizes up the situation, steps into the street carefully but confidently, gives a blast on his whistle, and stretches out his hand—and the cars stop. There's no doubt in his mind that he's in control in that intersection because he has a settled belief in his authority.

As a Christian, if you don't believe you have authority, you're not going to exercise it. If your belief is weak, your expression of it will also be weak and ineffective. But if you have a confident grip on the authority that Christ has given you, you will exercise it with confidence.

I (Neil) received an interesting phone call one night from a youth pastor whose belief in his authority was being put to the test. He was visiting at the home of one of the young people in his church while the parents were out bowling. It was a Christian family, but an older brother in the home had been living a lie. He was deceiving his family members and was being deceived.

"Dr. Anderson, I was sitting here visiting with a kid from my group and his little sister when we sensed an evil presence in the room. It scared us all. I knew something was very wrong."

"What did you do?" I asked.

"I said out loud, 'All right, I know you're here. Show yourself to us.' Suddenly a picture on the wall turned 90 degrees. That's when I decided to call you."

My young friend's belief in his authority had suddenly worn thin. If you ever challenge an evil spirit the way he did, you need to be able to exercise your authority in Christ and resolve the conflict.

I went to the house the next night and met with the whole family, including the boy whose lying ways had opened the door for demonic activity. We prayed together, and the father, as head of the household, took authority over their home and committed it and his family to the Lord.

For two days there was no evidence of an evil presence. Then one night the enemy apparently decided to test the family's faith. The little girl woke up in the middle of the night terrified. She saw an eerie light in the hallway shining under her bedroom door. Her parents were asleep across the hall, and she wanted to go to them, but she was afraid to open the door. Finally, remembering our prayer time a few nights earlier, she exercised her belief and opened the door. As soon as she did, the light was gone, never to return.

You may consider yourself just a "rookie" at stopping the devil's traffic in your life. But Jesus Christ is a seasoned veteran, and you're in Him. Build your faith in your authority by studying how Jesus operated against the powers of darkness in the Gospels and how we are commanded to do so in the Epistles.

2. *Humility*. Humility doesn't mean that you're always looking for a rock to crawl under because you feel unworthy to do anything. Humility is confidence that is properly placed. In exercising our authority, humility is placing confidence in Christ, the source of our authority, instead of in ourselves. Jesus didn't shrink back from exercising His authority, but He showed tremendous humility because He did everything according to what His Father told Him to do.

Pride says, "I resisted the devil all by myself." False humility says, "God resisted the devil; I did nothing." True humility says, "I resisted the devil by the grace of God." Apart from Christ we can do *nothing* (John 15:5), but that doesn't mean we're not supposed to do *something*. We exercise authority humbly in His strength and in His name.

3. *Boldness*. A Spirit-controlled Christian has a true, godly sense of courage and boldness in spiritual warfare. Just before entering the Promised Land, Joshua was challenged four times to be strong and courageous (Joshua 1:6,7,9,18). When the early church prayed about its mission of sharing the gospel in Jerusalem, "the place where they had gathered together was shaken, and they were all filled with the Holy Spirit and began to speak the word of God with boldness" (Acts 4:31). Spirit-inspired boldness is behind every successful advance in the church today.

The opposite of boldness is cowardice, fear, and unbelief. Notice what God thinks about these characteristics:

> I am the Alpha and Omega, the beginning and the end. I will give to the one who thirsts from the spring of the water of life without cost. He who overcomes will inherit these things, and I will be his God and he will be My son. But for the cowardly and unbelieving and abominable and murderers and immoral persons and sorcerers and idolaters and all liars, their part will be in the lake that burns with fire and brimstone, which is the second death (Revelation 21:6-8).

That's pretty serious—the cowardly and unbelieving lined up at the lake of fire alongside murderers, sorcerers, and idolaters! It should serve to motivate us to believe God and boldly live a righteous life: "God has not given us a spirit of timidity, but of power and love and discipline" (2 Timothy 1:7).

A lot of Christians fear the dark side of the spiritual world. They say, "I'm afraid to talk about demons." It's true that a little knowledge can be a dangerous and frightful thing, but a growing knowledge of the truth is liberating.

4. *Dependence.* The authority we're talking about here is not an independent authority. We don't charge out on our own like some kind of Christian ghostbusters to hunt down the devil and engage him in combat. God's primary call is for each of us to focus on the ministry of the kingdom: loving, caring, preaching, teaching, praying, and so on. However, when demonic powers challenge us in the course of pursuing this ministry, we deal with them on the basis of our authority in Christ and our dependence on Him. This

authority is not over each other, for we are to "be subject to one another in the fear of Christ" (Ephesians 5:21). It is over the kingdom of darkness. Light dispels darkness. Truth exposes the lie.

The Bottom Line: Freedom

When we boldly and humbly exercise the authority that Christ has given us over spiritual powers, we experience the freedom from bondage which Christ promised (John 8:32). It's a freedom that secular counseling usually can't produce, as a counselor named Barry discovered.

Christy, a young woman, came to my (Neil's) friend Barry because of the horrible abuse she suffered growing up. Barry dealt with Christy's problems with her family and friends, and Christy followed his suggestions. But she didn't get any better. After working with Christy for nearly four years, Barry brought her to me.

"Tell me about your childhood friends, Christy," I probed.

"The only other girl on our block lived across the street from me, so we were friends."

"What was her family like?"

Christy lowered her eyes. "Her mother did strange things in their home," she almost whispered.

"Did these strange things involve candles and sacrifices, sometimes even killing animals?"

"Yeah."

By this time Barry's eyes were as big as silver dollars. In nearly four years of counseling, Christy had never told him that a witch lived across the street from her as a child.

"Were you ever required to take off your clothes during these rituals?" Christy nodded. "And were there others there, men and women, who took off their clothes and performed sexual acts with you and each other?" Again she nodded.

Christy's neighbor finally moved away. But every night a demonic manifestation of this witch appeared to her in her room and talked with her. I led Christy through the Steps to Freedom, and she exercised her authority in Christ and dismissed the evil influence from her life. It came back occasionally, and sometimes Christy failed to stand against it because she was "just tired of fighting the battle." But when she stood her ground on Christ's authority, she was free.

Satan can do nothing about your position in Christ. But if he can, he will cloud your beliefs and confuse you, trying to make you forget who you are in Christ. This is how he tears down your faith and defeats you in spiritual battle.

We want to echo Paul's prayer in Ephesians 1. We pray that your eyes will be opened so you can see and understand the authority and power that Christ has extended to you as a believer.

Truth Encounter

Read:
Matthew 28:18; Luke 10:17

Reflect:

1. Jesus gave His followers power and authority over demonic forces. What's the difference between power and authority?

2. Do teenage Christians have the same authority and power over the demonic as the first followers of Jesus?

3. What four qualities need to be present in our lives to make God's authority available to us?

4. Since Satan can do nothing about our position in Christ, how will he try to defeat us in spiritual battle?

Respond:

Pray that your eyes will be opened so that you can see and understand the power and authority that Christ has extended to you.

Jesus Has You Covered

SIX

HAVE YOU EVER SAID TO YOURSELF, "I've had *more* trouble in my life since I became a Christian"? A lot of Christians have made that discovery. Why is being a Christian sometimes so tough? Because when we became God's children, we gained an enemy we didn't have before. In our B.C. days (before Christ), the devil didn't have to bother us because we were already part of his kingdom. His goal was to keep us there by blinding us to God's plan of salvation (2 Corinthians 4:3,4).

But when we came to life in Christ, Satan didn't curl up his tail and pull in his fangs. He is still committed to fouling up our life with his lies so he can "prove" that Christianity doesn't work, that God's Word isn't true, and that nothing really happened when we were born again.

So what's the benefit of being a Christian? Who in his right mind would want to sign up for a life of trouble? you may wonder. In reality, it doesn't need to be a life of trouble. We don't have to be a defenseless hockey puck at the mercy of Satan and his demons. God has already supplied the protection we need to ward off any and every satanic attack. We just need to know what God has provided and apply it in our own lives.

Some young Christians are a little paranoid about evil powers. They fear that demons are waiting around every corner to possess them. That's an unreal fear. Our relationship to demonic powers in the spiritual world is a lot like our relationship to germs in the physical world. We know that germs are all around us: in the air, in the water, in our food, in other people, even in us. But do we live in constant fear of catching some disease? No—unless we're hypochondriacs! We should know enough about healthy living to eat the right foods, get enough rest, and keep ourselves clean. Don't be germ-conscious. Be health-conscious, and your immune system will protect you. If you happen to catch a cold or get the measles, simply deal with it and go on with your life.

It's the same in the spiritual world. Demons are like little invisible germs looking for someone to infect. We are never told in the Bible to be afraid of them. We just need to be aware that they are real and commit ourselves to live a righteous life in spite of them. Should we come under attack, we deal with it and go on with life. Don't be demon-centered; be Christ-centered.

Remember: The only thing big about a demon is its mouth. Demons are habitual liars. In Jesus Christ the Truth, we are equipped with all the authority and protection we need to deal with anything they throw at us.

Getting Involved in God's Protection

Ephesians 6:10-18 tells us all about God's protection program. Notice how often we are commanded to be actively involved in the spiritual defense that He has provided for us:

> Finally, *be strong* in the Lord and in the strength of His might. *Put on* the full armor of God, so that you will *be able* to *stand firm* against the schemes of the devil. For our struggle is not against flesh

and blood, but against the rulers, against the powers, against the world forces of this darkness, against the spiritual forces of wickedness in the heavenly places. Therefore, *take up* the full armor of God, so that you will be *able* to *resist* in the evil day, and having done everything, to *stand firm* (verses 10-13, emphasis added).

You may be wondering, *If my position in Christ is secure and my protection is found in Him, why do I have to get involved? Can't I just kick back and let Him protect me?*

That's like a soldier saying, "Our country has a big, powerful army. We have the most advanced tanks and planes in the world. Why should I bother with wearing a helmet or learning to shoot a gun? I'll just stay in camp while the tanks and planes fight the war." When the enemy troops appear, guess which soldier will get shot first!

God, our "commanding officer," has provided everything we need to win the battle against the evil forces of darkness. But He says, "I've prepared a winning battle plan and designed effective weapons. But if you don't do your part by staying on active duty, you're likely to become a casualty." You can't expect God to protect you from demonic influences if you don't take an active part in His prepared strategy.

Dressed for Battle

The armor that God has provided for us and has instructed us to wear is our main protection from the enemy. Paul wrote:

> Stand firm then, with the belt of truth buckled around your waist, with the breastplate of righteousness in place, and with your feet fitted with

> the readiness that comes from the gospel of peace.
> In addition to all this, take up the shield of faith,
> with which you can extinguish all the flaming
> arrows of the evil one. Take the helmet of salva-
> tion and the sword of the Spirit, which is the word
> of God (Ephesians 6:14-17 NIV).

When we put on the armor of God, we are really putting on Christ (Romans 13:12-14). And when we put on Christ, we put ourselves under Christ's protection, where the evil one cannot touch us (1 John 5:18).

Armor You Have Already Put On

It appears from Ephesians 6:14,15 that we are already wearing three of the pieces of armor: the belt, breastplate, and shoes. These pieces of armor represent the protection given to us when we received Jesus Christ. We are not commanded to put these pieces on but to stand firm in them.

The belt of truth. Jesus said, "I am the...truth" (John 14:6). And because Christ is in us, the truth is in us. However, continuing to choose truth is not always easy. Since Satan's main weapon is the lie, our belt of truth (which holds the other pieces of body armor in place) is continually being attacked. If Satan can disable us in the area of truth, we become an easy target for his other attacks.

We stand firm in the truth by relating everything we do to the truth of God's Word. If a thought comes to mind that doesn't go along with God's truth, kick it out. If an opportunity comes along to say or do something that compromises or conflicts with the truth, avoid it. Adopt a simple rule of behavior: If it's the truth, I'm in; if it's not the truth, count me out.

The breastplate of righteousness. When we put on Christ at salvation we were forgiven and justified, and we became partakers of Christ's divine nature (2 Peter 1:4). It's not *our* righteousness but Christ's (1 Corinthians 1:30; Philippians 2:8,9). So when Satan aims an arrow at you by saying, "You're not good enough to be a Christian," you can respond with Paul, "Who will bring any charge against those whom God has chosen? It is God who justifies" (Romans 8:33 NIV). Your position in Christ is your protection against Satan's accusations that you're nothing but a worthless sinner.

Even though we're happy about our position of righteousness in Christ, we are well aware that we sometimes think, say, or do things we shouldn't. We are saints who sin. Standing firm in our righteousness involves understanding and applying what God's Word says about confession.

God's remedy for sin is stated in 1 John 1:9: "If we confess our sins, He is faithful and righteous to forgive us our sins and to cleanse us from all unrighteousness." Confession is different from saying, "I'm sorry," or asking forgiveness. To confess means to agree with God.

Suppose when you were younger your father caught you throwing a rock at a car. Dad says, "You threw a rock at a car, and that was wrong." If you respond, "I'm sorry, Dad," have you confessed? Not really. You may also say, "Please forgive me, Dad," but have you confessed yet? No. You haven't confessed until you agree with your dad and say, "I threw a rock at a car. I was wrong."

When we sin we may feel sorry, but feeling sorry or even telling God we're sorry isn't confession. We confess our sin when we say what God says about it: "I thought about that girl (or guy) with lust, and that's a sin"; "I got angry and yelled at my brother this morning, and that was wrong";

"pride motivated me to seek that student council position, and pride doesn't belong in my life."

Satan will make confession as difficult for you as he can. He will try to convince you that it's too late for confession, that God has already erased your name out of the Lamb's book of life. That's another one of his big lies. You're in Christ; you're already forgiven. You are righteous in Christ (2 Corinthians 5:21), and He will never leave you. Your relationship with God is not at stake when you sin, but your daily victory is. Your confession of sin clears the way for you to live a righteous life day by day.

The shoes of peace. When we receive Christ we are united with the Prince of Peace. We have peace *with* God right now (Romans 5:1), but the peace *of* Christ must also rule in our heart. That is possible only when we fill our heart daily with God's Word (Colossians 3:15,16).

The shoes of peace become protection against the many schemes of the devil when you act as a peacemaker among believers (Romans 14:19). Peacemakers bring people together by promoting fellowship and by bringing divided Christians together. Preserve Christian unity by being a peacemaker in your relationships (Matthew 5:9; Ephesians 4:3).

The Rest of the Armor

Paul mentions three more pieces of armor that we must put on to protect ourselves from Satan's attack: the shield of faith, the helmet of salvation, and the sword of the Spirit, which is the Word of God. The first three pieces of armor are the result of our position in Christ; the last three help us continue to win the battle.

The shield of faith. Faith is simply what you believe about God and His Word. The more you know about God and His

Word, the more faith you will have. The less you know, the smaller your shield of faith will be and the easier it will be for one of Satan's fiery arrows to hit you. If you want your shield of faith to grow large and provide greater protection from Satan, you need to increase your knowledge of God and His Word (Romans 10:17).

These flaming arrows from Satan are nothing more than smoldering lies, burning accusations, and fiery temptations bombarding our minds. When a deceptive thought, accusation, or temptation enters your mind, meet it head-on with what you know to be true about God and His Word. How did Jesus deflect Satan's temptation? By shielding Himself with statements from the Word of God. Every time you memorize a Bible verse, listen to a sermon, or participate in a Bible study at youth group, you increase your knowledge of God and enlarge your shield of faith. We are not called to dispel the darkness; we are called to turn on the light. You overcome a lie by choosing the truth.

The helmet of salvation. If your shield of faith is a little leaky and your daily victory difficult to achieve, be confident that the helmet of salvation guarantees your eternal victory. The helmet also covers the most important part of your body: your mind, where spiritual battles are either won or lost. As you struggle with the world, the flesh, and the devil on a daily basis, stand firm knowing that your salvation does not come and go with your successes and failures. You are a child of God, and nothing can separate you from the love of Christ (Romans 8:38,39).

The sword of the Spirit. The Word of God is the only offensive weapon mentioned in the list of armor. In this verse, Paul seems to be referring to the spoken Word of God. We are to defend ourselves against the evil one by speaking aloud God's truth.

Why is it so important to speak God's Word in addition to believing it and thinking it? Because Satan doesn't perfectly know what we're thinking. He is a created being; he can't read our thoughts like God can. If we only tell Satan to leave with our thoughts, he may not leave because he can't hear us. *We must stand against direct attacks by speaking out.*

Many students whom we have helped at our "Stomping Out the Darkness" student conferences share a common experience. They state that they were awakened in the middle of the night absolutely terrified for no apparent reason. It was a fear that made their skin crawl, and they knew it was an attack from Satan. Because they had learned who they were in Christ and had learned about the nature of Satan's attacks, they simply applied the two-step remedy suggested by James: "Submit therefore to God. Resist the devil and he will flee from you" (4:7). They were able to go back to sleep in complete peace.

Even my (Dave's) three-year-old daughter Dani learned to send the enemy running by speaking out on the authority of God's Word. After my wife, Grace, and I joined Freedom in Christ Youth Ministries, Dani began sensing an evil presence in her room at night—a creature she called "Ugly Sun" with four others she called monkeys. She knew they were bad, and she was terrified by their presence.

One night we heard her crying. As we entered her room, she said the creatures were there. She was so scared she literally tried to crawl inside Grace's pajamas to hide. We coached Dani in a prayer, and even though she was scared, she repeated after us these simple words: "By the power and the blood of Jesus, all the evil ones must leave."

Then Dani looked up, smiled, and with complete calmness said, "They're gone." She crawled under her covers and was asleep again in just a few minutes.

Age and physical strength have nothing to do with success in spiritual warfare (2 Corinthians 10:4); it is the Lord's strength that sends evil spirits running for cover. The power is in the spoken Word.

The Protective Power of Prayer

One young girl I (Dave) know saw God work in a powerful way through prayer. Julie's parents had been divorced for more than ten years, and her mother was heavily involved in the New Age movement. For as long as she could remember, her parents had never had a kind word for each other, and it was breaking her heart. Julie's mother also constantly put her down, telling her that she couldn't love her because she was overweight. She wasn't even allowed to call her own mother "Mom." She had to call her by her first name. Julie desperately wanted to be loved and accepted by her mother and wanted her parents to be kind to each other.

The situation was so bad that Julie was even afraid to pray about it. She figured that it really wasn't fair to ask God to do something so hard. I encouraged her that nothing is impossible or too hard for God. We prayed for her mother that her mind would be a quiet place where God could speak to her and that she would not continue to discourage her daughter.

I received a phone call from Julie a few days after our prayer together. She was so excited she could hardly control herself. "Prayer works! Prayer really works!" she exclaimed. "My mother just called a short time ago and she actually talked to my dad! They were even kind to each other. She then spoke with me, and she said she wanted to just call me up and say how proud she was that I was her daughter and that she loved me. Isn't God awesome? Prayer is powerful!"

One of the most dramatic conversions I (Neil) have observed happened in a man who professed to be a high priest in Satanism. Six months after he was set free, he gave his testimony in our church. At the close of his testimony I asked him, "Based on your experience on 'the other side,' what is the Christian's first line of defense against demonic influence?"

"Prayer," he answered forcefully. "And when you pray, mean it. Fervent prayer blocks Satan's activity like nothing else."

We never know completely the effects of our prayers. But we do know that God includes our prayer as part of His strategy for establishing His kingdom. After instructing us to put on the armor that God has provided, Paul wrote: "Pray all the time. Ask God for anything in line with the Holy Spirit's wishes. Plead with him, reminding him of your needs, and keep praying earnestly for all Christians everywhere" (Ephesians 6:18 TLB).

What is prayer? It is communication with God. God knows what we need in our battle with the powers of darkness, and He is more ready to meet our needs than we are to ask. Asking God demonstrates our dependence on Him.

In humility we pray, "You are the Lord, not I. You know what's best; I don't. I'm not telling You what to do; I'm asking. I declare my dependence on You." Such prayers open the way for God to act on our behalf.

Praying for Spiritual Sight

There are several specific needs we should pray about in spiritual warfare. One target of our prayers is the blindness Satan has caused in unbelievers (2 Corinthians 4:3,4). People cannot come to Christ unless their spiritual eyes are opened.

Prayer is a primary weapon in combating spiritual blindness. The apostle John wrote: "If we ask anything according to His will, He hears us. And if we know that He hears us in whatever we ask, we know that we have the requests which we have asked from Him" (1 John 5:14,15). Then he immediately challenged believers to apply what they learned by asking God to bring life to unbelievers (verse 16). Our strategy for bringing others to Christ must include prayer that God's light would penetrate the blindness caused by Satan.

We also need to pray, as Paul did in Ephesians 1:18,19, that the eyes of believers may be opened to understand our spiritual power, authority, and protection in Christ. As long as Satan can keep us in the dark about our position and authority in Christ, our growth, witness, and service as Christians will be severely limited. We need to pray for each other continually that Satan's smokescreen of lies will be blown away and that our vision into the spiritual world will be crystal-clear.

Binding the Strong Man

Another target for prayer is the "strong man" whom Jesus talked about in Matthew 12:29. Referring to Satan and his demons Jesus said, "How can anyone enter the strong man's house and carry off his property, unless he first binds the strong man?" He was saying that you can't rescue people from the chains of spiritual blindness or demonic influence unless you first overpower their captors. Satan's power is already broken, but he won't let go of anything until we exercise our authority in Christ.

When we pray against the strong man, we grab onto what rightfully belongs to God and hold on until Satan turns loose. He will hold onto these people until we demand their release on the basis of our authority in Christ. Once Satan is bound through prayer, he must let go.

Several years ago a personal experience emphasized to me (Neil) the power of prayer in dealing with people who are in the clutches of the strong man. A man named Bill came to my office one Sunday afternoon. I barely knew him, and I didn't have much time to chat. But I was concerned about him, so I began, "I'm glad you're here, Bill. May I ask you a personal question?" Bill nodded. "Have you ever trusted in Christ to be your Lord and your Savior?"

"No."

"Would you like to?"

"I don't know, Neil," Bill answered with a slightly troubled expression.

I brought out a salvation tract and read through it with him. "Do you understand this, Bill?"

"Yes."

"Would you like to make that decision for Christ now?"

"Yes."

"I'll pray a simple prayer of commitment, and you repeat it after me phrase by phrase, okay?"

"Okay."

"Lord Jesus, I need you," I began.

Bill began to respond, "Lor-r-r..." Then he locked up completely. I realized that I had invaded the territory of the strong man, Satan, and he didn't want to let go of Bill.

"Bill, there's a battle going on for you," I said. "I'm going to read some Scripture and pray out loud for you. I'm going to bind the enemy and stand against him. As soon as you can, you just tell Jesus what you believe." His eyes told me that the battle within him was raging.

I started reading Scripture and praying aloud every prayer I could think of to bind Satan and set Bill free. After several minutes of prayer and Scripture, Bill suddenly groaned, "Lord Jesus, I need You." Then he slumped back in his chair like he had just gone ten rounds with the world heavyweight champion. He looked at me with tear-filled eyes and said, "I'm free." I had never used the word "freedom" with him; that was his expression. But he was free, and he knew it.

God has equipped you with everything you need to ward off the attack of the devil in your life. And He has also equipped you for and authorized you to perform "search and rescue" in the lives of those who are in the strong man's clutches. Stand firm in the armor that God has provided, and step out in Christ's authority to rob the strong man's house for God.

Truth Encounter

Read
Read:

Ephesians 6:10-18

Reflect
Reflect:

1. Many young Christians often have more trouble in their lives after they accept Christ than before. Why do you think this might be true?

2. Which of the six pieces of God's armor do you think you need to focus on in your spiritual conflicts at home, school, and with friends?

3. In the midst of a spiritual conflict, have you ever doubted your salvation? Why is it important to understand that your salvation is an eternal possession?

4. What are the two areas of prayer talked about in this chapter? Have you ever prayed for someone regarding these areas? What were the results?

Respond
Respond:

After reading Ephesians 6:10-18, decide to put the armor of God into action. Pray out loud as you review each piece you already have on and as put on each of the other pieces. Also ask God to reveal to your mind those people you know who are blinded in their unbelief. Make a list of their names as they come to mind, and pray for their salvation daily.

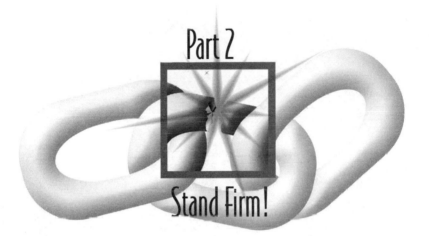

Part 2

Stand Firm!

Dealing with Evil

SEVEN

WE LIVE IN A WORLD THAT IS under the authority of an evil ruler. Originally God created Adam and his race to rule over creation. But Adam gave up his position of authority through sin, and Satan became the rebel holder of authority. Jesus called him "the ruler of this world" (John 12:31; 14:30; 16:11).

Satan ruled from Adam until the cross. The death, resurrection, and ascension of Christ secured the final authority forever for Jesus Himself (Matthew 28:18). That authority was given to all believers in the Great Commission so that we could continue undoing the work of the evil one (1 John 3:8).

Living on the Enemy's Turf

We were all born spiritually dead, slaves of the ruler of this world. But when we received Christ, God "rescued us out of the darkness and gloom of Satan's kingdom and brought us into the Kingdom of his dear Son" (Colossians 1:13 TLB). We're now citizens of a different place. Satan still rules this world, but he's not *our* ruler anymore because Jesus is our Lord.

But as long as we remain on planet earth, we are still on Satan's turf. He's going to try to fool us into believing that we're still under his authority, and he'll try to rule our lives. Who can protect us from this evil tyrant? Only Christ. Not only has Christ provided protection for us, but in Him we have authority over the kingdom of darkness. On top of that, we have the Holy Spirit living in us. He's the Spirit of truth, and He will be our Guide into all truth (John 14:17; 16:13).

How Vulnerable Are We?

We are secure in Christ, and we have all the protective armor we could ever need. But we're still vulnerable to Satan's accusations, temptations, and deceptions (see Figure 7a). We know this because God has told us to put on His armor—and why would we need the armor unless Satan could get to us without it?

It's likely that every believer will be influenced in some way by the devil. He can get some sort of control over us if he can fool us into believing his lies. We have seen many young Christians who are almost stopped dead by Satan's

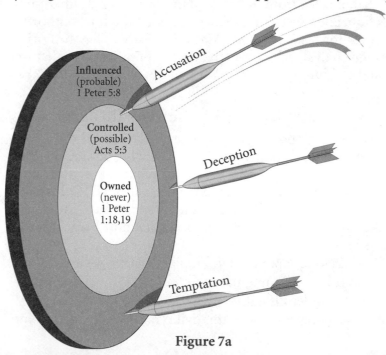

Figure 7a

deception. They're so oppressed that they can't seem to make the right choices and live responsible lives. Even though they actually *can* make choices, they don't *think* they can, and so they don't.

Our *ownership* is never at stake, though. We belong to God forever, and the evil one can never touch who we are in Christ. We are always "Holy Spirit–possessed." But as long as we're living in our natural bodies here on the devil's turf, we're the target for Satan's fiery darts. This is reality. We can't just stick our heads in the sand like an ostrich, because if we do, we're leaving an incredibly vulnerable target exposed.

The Powers That Be

Most Christians agree that Satan is a living being who is mostly responsible for the evil in the world. But when you start talking about demons being alive and active in the world, a lot of Christians resist: "Hold on there. I believe in the devil, but I don't buy that stuff about demons."

Think about it: How does Satan carry on his worldwide ministry of evil and deception? He is a created being. He isn't all-knowing or all-powerful. He can't be everywhere in the world, tempting and deceiving millions of people at the same moment. He does it through an army of spiritual beings (demons, evil spirits, fallen angels, and so on) who carry out his plan of rebellion throughout the world.

Perhaps the best description of the evil spiritual army that harasses God's people is found in Ephesians 6:12: "Our struggle is not against flesh and blood, but against the rulers, against the powers, against the world forces of this darkness, against the spiritual forces of wickedness in the heavenly places." It is clear from the verses surrounding Ephesians

6:12 that the rulers, powers, and forces which oppose us are spiritual beings in the spiritual world.

We have been targeted by demons numerous times. However, it's not a frightening experience for us, and it shouldn't be for you. John declared, "Greater is He who is in you than he who is in the world" (1 John 4:4). You have authority over Satan's activity, and you have the armor of God to protect you. Whenever Satan attacks, you must "be strong in the Lord and in the strength of His might" (Ephesians 6:10). Consciously place yourself in the Lord's hands, and resist Satan by speaking God's Word. You are only open to the devil's arrows when you are walking by sight instead of by faith or walking in the flesh instead of in the Spirit.

What should we do about Satan's hierarchy of demonic powers? Nothing! We are not to be demon-centered; we are to be God-centered and ministry-centered. We are to fix our eyes on Jesus, share the gospel, love one another, and be God's ambassadors in our fallen world.

The Personality of Demons

The Bible does not attempt to prove the existence of demons any more than it attempts to prove the existence of God. It simply reports on their activities as though its readers accept their existence. Nor did the early church leaders have a problem with the reality and personality of demons (that is, the existence of demons as personal beings).

Luke 11:24-26 gives us a helpful view into the character of evil spirits. After Jesus cast out a demon that had made a man unable to speak, His enemies accused Him of casting out demons by the power of "Beelzebul, the ruler of the demons" (Luke 11:15). During the discussion about demons that followed, Jesus said:

> When the unclean spirit goes out of a man, it passes through waterless places seeking rest, and not finding any, it says, "I will return to my house from which I came." And when it comes, it finds it swept and put in order. Then it goes and takes along seven other spirits more evil than itself, and they go in and live there; and the last state of that man becomes worse than the first (verses 24-26).

We can learn several things about evil spirits from this passage.

1. *Demons can exist outside or inside humans.* Demons seem to want a home in a living being. A group of them once asked Jesus to send them into a herd of pigs (Mark 5:12). Some spirits apparently stay in certain geographical locations that have been used for satanic purposes. Satan and demons are spirits. In order to rule in the physical world, they need willing subjects to do their bidding. Deceived people are actually doing the work of Satan. God also is spirit (John 4:24), and he accomplishes His will on planet Earth by working through the church, His people.

2. *Demons are able to travel at will.* As spiritual beings, demons are not subject to the barriers of the natural world. The walls of your church building do not make it safe from demonic influence; only prayer and spiritual authority can do that.

3. *Demons are able to communicate.* It is obvious from Luke 11 that evil spirits can communicate with each other. They can also speak to humans through a person, as they did through the demon-possessed man in Mark 5:1-20.

4. *Each demon has a separate identity.* Notice the use of personal pronouns in Luke 11: "I will return to my house from which I came" (verse 24). We are dealing with thinking

personalities, not just a force. That's why worldly methods of research are not going to reveal the existence of evil spirits. The Bible alone is our source about their reality and personality.

5. *Demons are able to remember and make plans.* The fact that demons can leave a place, come back, remember what happened earlier, and plan reentry with others shows their ability to think and plan.

6. *Demons are able to evaluate situations and make decisions.* The fact that the evil spirit found its human target "swept and put in order" (verse 25) shows that a demon can evaluate its intended victim. Demons gain access to our lives through our points of weakness.

7. *Demons are able to combine forces.* In Luke 11, one spirit joined with a group of seven others, making things far worse for the victim. In Mark 5, so many demons ganged up on one man that he called himself "Legion" (verse 9), which refers to a large group of soldiers.

8. *Demons vary in degrees of wickedness.* The first demon in Luke 11 brought back seven other spirits "more evil than itself" (verse 26). Jesus indicated a difference in the wickedness of spirits when He said of one, "This kind cannot come out by anything but prayer" (Mark 9:29). The idea of differences in power and wickedness fits the levels that Paul lists in Ephesians 6:12.

You don't need to fear Satan and his demons as long as you cling to God's truth. If you keep on walking in the light, you don't have to be afraid of the darkness.

Dealing with the Evil Around Us

How do these evil spirits interfere with our lives? Here's a simple illustration. Imagine that you are standing at one end of a long, narrow street lined on both sides with two-story houses. At the other end of the street stands Jesus Christ. Your Christian life is the process of walking down that long street of maturity in Him. There is absolutely nothing in the street that can keep you from reaching Jesus. So when you receive Christ, you fix your eyes on Him and start walking.

But since this world is still under the control of Satan, the rows of houses on either side of the street are filled with beings who are committed to keeping you from reaching your goal. They have no power or authority to block your path or even slow your step. So they hang out of the windows and call to you, hoping to turn your attention away from your goal and disrupt your progress.

One of the ways they will try to distract you is by calling out, "Hey, look over here! I've got something you really want. It tastes good, feels good, and is a lot more fun than your boring walk down the street. Come on in and take a look." That's temptation—suggesting to your mind ways to serve yourself instead of God. We will talk more about temptation in Chapter 9.

As you continue your walk toward Christ, you will also have thoughts like "I'm stupid. I'm ugly. I'll never amount to anything for God." Satan's demons are masters at accusation, especially after they have distracted you through temptation. One minute they're saying, "Try this; there's nothing wrong with it." Then, when you give in to temptation, they're right there taunting, "See what you did! How can you call yourself a Christian when you behave like that?" Accusation is one of Satan's primary weapons in his attempt to distract us from our goal. We will talk about his strategy of accusation in Chapter 10.

Other messages that are thrown at you as you walk down the street sound like this: "You don't need to go to youth group today. It's not important to pray and read the Bible every day. Some of that New Age stuff isn't so bad." That's deception, and it is Satan's most powerful and crippling weapon.

The devil will often introduce these messages as if it were *us* thinking them: *"I* don't need to go to youth group today, pray, read my Bible," and so on. Satan knows we will be more easily deceived if he can make us think the thought was ours instead of his. We'll discuss Satan's strategy of deception in Chapter 11.

What is the enemy's goal in having his demons jeer at you, taunt you, lure you, and question you from the windows and doorways along your path? He wants you to slow down, stop, sit down, and if possible, give up your journey toward Christ. He wants to influence you to doubt your ability to believe and serve God. Remember: He has absolutely no power or authority to keep you from steadily moving forward in your walk toward Christ. And he can never again own you, because you have been redeemed by Jesus Christ and you are forever in Him (1 Peter 1:18,19).

But if he can get you to listen to the thoughts he plants in your mind, he can influence you. And if you allow him to influence you long enough through temptation, accusation, and deception, he can stop your progress. We'll talk more about how much the devil can influence a Christian in Chapter 12.

Levels of Bondage

There are several levels of spiritual freedom and bondage. On one side is the apostle Paul, whose Christian life and ministry were a great example despite his battle with sin and Satan (Romans 7:15-25; 2 Corinthians 12:7-9). On the other side is the man called Legion, who was totally controlled by demons (Mark 5:1-20).

Nobody loses control to Satan overnight; it's a gradual process of being deceived and yielding to his subtle influence. From what we have seen, no more than 15 percent of all Christian youth are completely free of Satan's bondage. These are the kids who are consistently living a Spirit-filled life and bearing fruit. The others are struggling along at one of three levels of spiritual conflict.

First, a believer may lead a fairly normal Christian life on the outside while wrestling with a steady stream of sinful thoughts on the inside: lust, envy, greed, hatred, apathy, and so on. This person has almost no devotional life. Prayer is a frustrating experience for him, and he usually struggles to get along with family and friends.

Most Christians in this condition have no idea that they are in the middle of a spiritual conflict. They might not say they are hearing voices but would quickly admit to having problems with controlling their thoughts. Instead of recognizing that their minds are being peppered by the fiery arrows of the enemy, they think the problem is their own fault. *If those bad thoughts are mine, what kind of person am I?* they wonder. So they end up condemning themselves while the enemy continues his attack. There are a huge number of Christians living at this level of spiritual conflict.

The second level of conflict is shown in those believers who see a difference between their own thoughts and strange, evil "voices" that seem to overpower them. *What am I thinking?* they wonder with alarm when sinful ideas, thoughts, and fantasies flood their minds. They experience no victory, and they are so afraid they're going crazy that they won't share their problem with anyone.

Yet the majority of Christians at this level also fail to see their struggle as a spiritual conflict. They seek counseling and try to control their thoughts, but they experience little or no improvement. Most of these people are depressed, anxious, paranoid, bitter, or angry, and may be addicted to alcohol, drugs, eating disorders, and so on.

At the third level of conflict, the person has lost all control. Voices inside his mind tell him what to think, say, and do. These people stay at home, wander the streets talking to imaginary people, or occupy beds in mental institutions or rehab units. Sadly, a small but significant number of Christians fall victim to this level of deception and control.

Just Say No

There are three ways of responding to the temptations, accusations, and deceptions demons throw at us during our daily walk with Christ, and two of these ways are wrong.

First, the most defeated young people are those who listen to demonic thoughts and believe them. An evil spirit whispers to them, "You don't pray, read your Bible, or witness like you should. How could God love you?" That's a huge lie because God's love is unconditional. But they start thinking about their failures and agreeing that they're probably not very lovable from God's point of view. Pretty soon they are sitting in the middle of the street going nowhere.

These Christians are totally defeated simply because they have been fooled into believing that God doesn't love them, or that they will never be victorious Christians, or that they are helpless victims of the past. There is no reason why they can't get up immediately and start walking again, but they have believed a lie, so they don't go anywhere.

The second response is just as worthless. We try to argue with the demons: "I am not ugly or stupid. I am a victorious Christian." We're proud that we don't believe what they say, but they're still telling us what to think and do. We're standing in the middle of the street shouting at them when we should be marching forward.

But it doesn't make any difference whether those lying thoughts come from demons, or the flesh, or the world. We obey Christ and take *every* thought captive. God didn't ask us to get rid of the darkness—He asked us to turn on the light.

I (Neil) dealt with a young woman who was stopped in her tracks by trying to fight negative demonic thoughts. After she was able to resolve her conflicts and gain her freedom in Christ, she wrote me this letter:

> What I've discovered this last week is this feeling of control. Like my mind is my own. I haven't sat and had these strung-out periods of thought and contemplation, that is, conversations with myself. My mind just simply feels quieted. It really is a strange feeling. My emotions have been stable. I haven't felt depressed once this week.
>
> For the first time, I believe I actually understand what it means to be a Christian, who Christ is, and who I am in Him. I feel capable of helping people and capable of handling myself. I guess I'm describing what it is like to be at peace. I feel this quiet, soft joy in my heart. Thank you for lending me your hope—I believe I have my own now in Christ.

This woman made the third kind of response to demonic thoughts, which is this: We overcome the world, the flesh, and the devil by *choosing the truth*. We are not to believe evil spirits, nor are we to talk with them. Instead, the right response is to ignore them. We are equipped with the armor of God; evil powers can't touch us unless we drop our guard. With every arrow of temptation, accusation, or deception they shoot at us, we simply raise the shield of faith, deflect the attack, and walk on (Colossians 2:6). Take every thought captive to the obedience of Christ. Choose truth in the face of every lie. As you do, you will find your maturity and freedom increasing with every step.

Truth Encounter

Read:

Ephesians 6:12; Luke 11:24-26

Reflect:

1. What are some of the ways young people picture Satan and demons? Do most young people believe that Satan and demons exist? What do you believe?

2. Can evil spirits put tempting thoughts in our minds? What are some of the ways we are tempted or distracted from following Christ?

3. What are some of the deceptive or accusing thoughts Satan might use against us? What deceptions has he placed in your mind?

4. Is it possible for Satan to gain control over a believer? What must be done to stop Satan's influence in our life?

Respond:

Nowhere in the Bible are we told to fear evil spirits or Satan. Pray and claim the protection and the authority you have in Christ. Thank God that Satan and his evil followers were defeated through Christ's death, burial, and resurrection. Pray out loud daily, "By the power and the blood of the Lord Jesus Christ, I command any and all evil to leave my presence."

The Lure of Knowledge and Power

HOW DO YOUNG PEOPLE GET trapped in the quicksand of Satan's control in the first place? What are some of the traps the devil has set to keep us from the freedom that is ours in Christ?

One of his major traps is his appeal to the human desire for spiritual knowledge and power. We crave a secret knowledge that is not normally available to the ordinary person. We want to experience a power that is spiritual and supernatural in origin. Satan knows this. That's why most occult groups and activities promise secret or special information or power that many people find hard to resist.

In a sense, the desire for knowledge and power is God-given. But it is intended to be fulfilled by the knowledge and power that comes from *God*. However, Satan is busy trying to pass off his counterfeits for God's knowledge and power as the real thing. If he can get you to accept his versions of knowledge and power, he has an open door into your life.

The lure of satanic knowledge and power is nothing new. God's people have been warned against it from the earliest times. Just before the nation of Israel entered Canaan, the Promised Land, Moses commanded them:

> You must be very careful lest you be corrupted by the horrible customs of the nations now living there. For example, any Israeli who presents his child to be burned to death as a sacrifice to heathen gods must be killed. No Israeli may practice black magic, or call on the evil spirits for aid, or be a fortune teller, or be a serpent charmer, medium,

or wizard, or call forth the spirits of the dead. Anyone doing these things is an object of horror and disgust to the Lord, and it is because the nations do these things that the Lord your God will displace them. You must walk blamelessly before the Lord your God (Deuteronomy 18:9-13 TLB).

This command is as viable for us today as it was for the Israelites under Moses' leadership. We live in a contemporary Canaan, where it is socially acceptable to consult spiritists, mediums, palm-readers, psychic counselors, and horoscopes for guidance and esoteric knowledge. This is unfortunately true among Christians also. During one of our student surveys we asked 1725 professing Christian

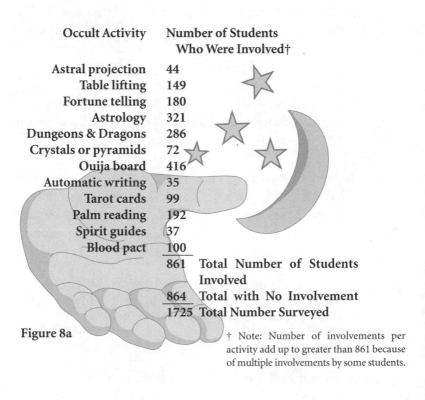

Occult Activity	Number of Students Who Were Involved†
Astral projection	44
Table lifting	149
Fortune telling	180
Astrology	321
Dungeons & Dragons	286
Crystals or pyramids	72
Ouija board	416
Automatic writing	35
Tarot cards	99
Palm reading	192
Spirit guides	37
Blood pact	100
861	Total Number of Students Involved
864	Total with No Involvement
1725	Total Number Surveyed

Figure 8a

† Note: Number of involvements per activity add up to greater than 861 because of multiple involvements by some students.

teenagers about their activity in the occult and discovered the following:*

Almost 50 percent of these Christian teenagers indicated some type of involvement! Some kids argue, "But this stuff really works. My horoscope is right on most of the time." The issue isn't whether or not it works, but whether or not it's right. According to God, it's *not* right, and we shouldn't be fooling around with it.

The darkest side of Satan's versions of spiritual knowledge and power mentioned by Moses—animal sacrifice, witchcraft, sorcery—is also thriving in our culture, though not as openly. It's still hard for some people to believe that young and old alike are actually worshipping Satan. But police departments are trying to tell your parents, "Wake up! Our kids are not just into drugs and illicit sex. They're into *Satanism*. We've seen the blood and the mutilated animals." It's getting so bad that one of the animal control agencies in our area will no longer release a black dog or cat for fear that it will become the victim of satanic abuse.

Every unthinkable act that Moses warned Israel not to get involved in—from horoscopes to animal and human sacrifice—is in place and operating in our culture today. And they all have their root in Satan's deception.

Knowledge from the Dark Side

Many people today are craving extra "hidden" knowledge about life. They don't want to hear what God has to say. They want information and direction from someone who "*knows*": a psychic, a channeler, a palm-reader, a card-reader, or the spirit of a dead friend or relative.

---

* Neil Anderson and Steve Russo, *The Seduction of Our Children* (Eugene, OR: Harvest House, 1991), pp. 34, 39.

The Bible is very clear about seeking knowledge and direction from anyone but God:

> Do not turn to mediums or spiritists; do not seek them out to be defiled by them....As for the person who turns to mediums and to spiritists, to play the harlot after them, I will also set My face against that person and will cut him off from among his people....A man or a woman who is a medium or a spiritist shall surely be put to death (Leviticus 19:31; 20:6,27).

In our country, we're about as far away from obeying that command as we can be. We have people channeling on TV and radio programs, and they're considered celebrities. One newspaper report stated that more women in Los Angeles visit spiritists than professional counselors. You can attend a psychic fair in practically any city in our land and get a personal spiritual "reading." The reader is either a fake or a spiritual medium who enters a trance and seemingly receives instruction for you from the spiritual world. Far from being seen as a black mark on society, these people are often revered as highly as doctors and ministers for their "expertise."

Mediums—Phony and for Real

Where do mediums and spiritists get their "amazing" information and insights? Many of them are being influenced by demons, but much of what is called spiritism or psychic activity is no more than a clever human trick. These so-called spiritists give what is referred to as "cold readings." You go to them for advice or direction, and they ask you a few simple questions. Based on the answers you give, they make general observations that are probably true of most people in your situation. But you are so impressed with the accuracy of their "revelations" that you start tipping them off about all kinds of details that they can then work into their "reading." This is not demonic; it's just a mental and verbal magic trick.

The mediums and spiritists that God warned against in Leviticus and Deuteronomy were not con artists, but people who possessed and passed on knowledge that didn't come just through clever observation. Such people have opened themselves up to the spirit world and have become channels of knowledge from Satan. The phony with his cold readings is interested only in taking your money. But the false knowledge and direction that comes from Satan through a medium is intended to rob you of your spiritual victory and freedom.

There's big money in these psychic/con artist operations, and a lot of magicians are raking it in. Many people crave to know something extra about their lives and their future, and they will pay well if they think someone can give them the inside information they desire.

The Down Side of Seeking the Dark Side

The Old Testament is full of examples of kings, false prophets, and mediums who led the nation of Israel in rebellion against God. One of the more well-known cases was Israel's first king. Saul began well by seeking God's guidance and was appointed by Samuel as king of Israel (1 Samuel 10). And he served well until his rebellion against God's will (1 Samuel 15), a sin which God says is the same as the sin of witchcraft (verse 23).

Why did Saul sin and reject the Word of the Lord? Because he feared the voice of the people more than the voice of God—a problem too many people struggle with in our world today. The problem of rebellion is the worst problem in the world.

Although Saul was sorry that he sinned (or at least sorry that he was caught!), there is no evidence to suggest that he really turned his back on his sinful ways. Like many people who disobey God, he tried to fix his mistake. But it was too late, and "the Spirit of the LORD departed from Saul, and an evil spirit from the LORD terrorized him" (1 Samuel 16:14).

This is a tough passage for two reasons. First, it seems to be saying that a person can lose the Holy Spirit by an act of disobedience. But we need to understand that the Holy Spirit in the Old Testament only came upon certain people at certain times for certain tasks. This unique equipping is not the same as the personal relationship with God through the Spirit that we enjoy as His children today.

Beginning after the cross, the church is identified by the indwelling presence of the Holy Spirit (Ephesians 1:13,14). Jesus promised that no one will snatch us out of His hand (John 10:28), and Paul assured that nothing—not even disobedience—can separate us from the love of God (Romans 8:35-39). We are secure in Christ, and the Spirit of Christ dwells in us through faith in the work of Christ on the cross. The Holy Spirit doesn't come and go in response to our obedience or disobedience.

The second problem concerns the troubling idea that an evil spirit could come from the Lord. But we must remember that God is supreme, and He can use Satan and his demons as a means to discipline His people as He did with Saul. This is no different from God using a godless nation like Assyria as "the rod of My anger" to discipline His people (Isaiah 10:5,6). God is God, and He can use demons to accomplish His will if He wants to.

Even the church is allowed to turn an immoral member over to Satan "to punish him, in the hope that his soul will be saved when our Lord Jesus Christ returns" (1 Corinthians 5:5 TLB). Why? So the world and its ruler, the devil, can do a number on such a person in order to bring about a real change.

Whenever the evil spirit came upon Saul, David would play his harp, and the evil spirit would depart (1 Samuel 16:23). How dense we are when it comes to understanding the biblical importance of music in the spiritual realm! During the reign of David, over 4000 musicians were assigned to sing in the temple night and day (1 Chronicles 9:33; 23:5). It is the mark of Spirit-filled Christians to sing and make melody in their hearts to the Lord and to speak to each other in psalms, hymns, and spiritual songs (Ephesians 5:18-20).

On the other side of the truth we find the destructive power of some secular music. The Satanist I (Neil) led to the Lord showed me numerous symbols on popular record albums indicating links to Satanism. He told me that about 85 percent of today's heavy metal and punk music groups are "owned" by Satanists. They have unwittingly sold themselves to Satanism in exchange for fame and fortune. Few of these artists actually practice Satanism, but most are hopelessly lost and lead others astray through the godless message in their music.

After Samuel the prophet died, Saul's twisted desire for spiritual knowledge led him to seek guidance from a medium—the witch of Endor. Coming to the witch in disguise, Saul persuaded her to call up the spirit of dead Samuel (1 Samuel 28:8-19). But the scheme backfired when God permitted Samuel himself to return, terrifying the witch. Samuel's message to Saul was nothing but bad news. He said that the

Philistines would defeat Israel and that Saul and his sons would be killed (verse 19). It happened just as Samuel said.

God clearly forbids communicating with the dead (Isaiah 8:19,20), and the story of the rich man and Lazarus teaches the present-day impossibility of communicating with the dead (Luke 16:19-31). When a psychic claims to have contacted the dead, don't believe it. When a psychologist claims to have taken a client back to a former life through hypnosis, don't believe it. When a New Age medium reports to have channeled a person from the past into the present, realize that this is nothing more than the work of a demon or the trick of a con artist.

An Old Idea in New Clothing

The thirst for knowledge and power has lured many youth to seek guidance from mediums and spiritists and through such occultic practices as fortune-telling, tarot cards, palm-reading, Ouija boards, astrology, magic charming, and automatic writing. "Is it because there is no God in Israel that you are going to inquire of Baal-zebub [Satan]?" Elijah lamented (2 Kings 1:3). Young people all around us are ignoring the God who promises to love them and guide them, and are instead seeking light and peace in the kingdom of darkness.

Don't be carried away by the prospect of knowledge and power that is luring so many youth in our culture away from God. Those who seek knowledge and power from the dark side will greatly interfere with the work of God, deceiving many by the counterfeit forces they employ. Other people will thirst after power to such an extent that they will even sacrifice their own children to demons (Psalm 106:36-38). We can verify firsthand from our counseling experience that these kinds of things are actually happening today.

Let these sad words from the Bible remind us that even believers can be lured away from the knowledge and power of God by our enemy. And let them encourage us to seek knowledge and power from God alone.

> But Israel was soon overfed; yes, fat and bloated; then, in plenty, they forsook their God. They shrugged away the Rock of their salvation. Israel began to follow foreign gods, and Jehovah was very angry; he was jealous of his people. They sacrificed to heathen gods, to new gods never before worshiped. They spurned the Rock who had made them, forgetting it was God who had given them birth (Deuteronomy 32:15-18 TLB).

Truth Encounter

Read:

Deuteronomy 18:9-13; 1 Samuel 15:23

Reflect:

1. Why should we be careful not to get involved with mediums or spiritists? What are some of the possible side effects that might follow if someone were to open himself or herself up to this kind of cultic activity?

2. Why is rebellion like the sin of divination or witchcraft? How does rebellion relate to arrogance?

3. How was music used in the worship of God in Old Testament times? Why must we carefully select the music we listen to?

4. What kind of New Age teaching or practices do you see in your school? On television? In your community? How can you avoid being drawn into New Age thinking in our world today?

Respond:

One of the big dangers we face is our curiosity about the New Age and occult practices. The lure of satanic knowledge and power is something God warns us to watch out for. Pray and ask God to help you cut off your craving for hidden knowledge or power. Ask God to reveal to your mind the practices you have been involved in, so that you can confess and renounce them.

Tempted to Do It Your Way

I (Dave) remember one of my earliest experiences with temptation. One day as young boys, two of my friends and I jumped on our bikes for a trip down to the local department store. It was a long ride, so we had time to talk. At first we discussed what we wanted to buy: packages of exploding caps made for cap guns. But as we neared the store, the conversation took a bad turn. We began to discuss how easy it would be to steal the caps. The idea of getting something for nothing was tempting, and we decided to do it.

We entered the store and went straight to the toy section. I was both excited and scared about the heist as each of my friends slipped a package of caps inside his pocket. Suddenly it was my turn, and they stepped aside to give me a clear view of the prize.

My heart was pounding so hard I thought it was going to explode in my chest. I knew taking the caps was wrong, but I didn't want to be labeled a chicken. So I reached for the them...then stopped. I remembered the hidden cameras. I glanced up at the huge, shiny bubble on the ceiling made of one-way glass. There was a camera inside that bubble. My brother-in-law worked at the store and had told me all about

135

the camera system. It would be crazy to try to steal something; we were being watched!

I sheepishly announced to my friends that I wasn't going to do it. They grumbled at me and called me a chicken, then we headed for the exit. Two men from store security suddenly blocked our escape. "Where are the caps, boys?" they asked, glaring at us.

"What caps?" my two friends replied in unison, faking their innocence.

"Come on, boys, we saw you take them," the security men fired back.

My two friends fell apart and cried like babies. I tried to hide my relief that I had chickened out at the last minute. It was one time in my life when, thanks to the grace of God and a security camera, I didn't yield to temptation.

In this chapter we want to talk about temptation so you can easily recognize it and quickly refuse Satan's invitation to do things your own way.

What Is Temptation?

Temptation is being enticed to have genuine needs met through the world, the flesh, and the devil instead of through Christ (Philippians 4:19). Every temptation is an invitation to do things our own way instead of God's way.

Most of us won't often be tempted to commit obvious sins like armed robbery, murder, or rape. Satan is too clever and sneaky for that. He knows that we will recognize obvious wrong and refuse to act on it. Instead, he likes to entice us to push something good beyond the boundary of the will of God until it becomes sin.

Paul wrote, "I can do anything I want to if Christ has not said no, but some of these things aren't good for me. Even if

I am allowed to do them, I'll refuse to if I think they might get such a grip on me that I can't easily stop when I want to" (1 Corinthians 6:12 TLB). Paul saw nothing but green lights in every direction of the Christian life. Everything is good and lawful for us because we are free from sin and no longer under the condemnation of the law. But Paul also knew that if we go 80 miles per hour in any of these good and lawful directions, we will eventually run the red light of God's will, and that's sin.

The following statements show the sinful results in a number of areas where we are tempted to take the good things that God created beyond the boundary of God's will:

- physical rest becomes laziness
- quietness becomes an unwillingness to talk to anyone
- ability to make money becomes greed
- enjoyment of life becomes too much partying, drinking, and so on
- physical pleasure becomes lust
- interest in the possessions of others becomes coveting
- enjoyment of food becomes gluttony
- taking good care of yourself becomes selfishness
- talking with others becomes gossip
- anger becomes rage and bad temper
- judgment becomes criticism
- same-sex friendship becomes homosexuality
- opposite-sex friendship becomes immorality
- generosity becomes wastefulness
- carefulness and caution become fear

Some Christians confuse temptation with sin. Temptation is not the same as sin. Even Jesus was "tempted in all things as we are." But finish the verse: "Yet without sin" (Hebrews 4:15). As long as we are in the world, we are exposed to temptation just like Jesus was. But He didn't sin, and we don't have to sin either (1 Corinthians 10:13). Temptation is like seeing Satan's face through the window; sin is like unlocking and opening the door, making it possible for him to come in. Remember, God's boundaries are not restrictive; they are protective.

Channels of Temptation

You will be better prepared to resist temptation in your life when you realize that, according to the Scriptures, there are only three channels through which Satan will entice you to act outside of God's will. They are talked about in 1 John 2:15-17:

> Do not love the world nor the things in the world. If anyone loves the world the love of the Father is not in him. For all that is in the world, the lust of the flesh and the lust of the eyes and the boastful pride of life, is not from the Father, but is from the world. The world is passing away, and also its lusts; but the one who does the will of God lives forever.

The three channels of temptation are the *lust of the flesh*, the *lust of the eyes*, and the *pride of life*. The lust of the flesh tempts us to fulfill our physical appetites (food, sex, comfort, and so on) in a sinful, worldly way. The lust of the eyes tempts us to do what we think is best instead of obeying the

Bible. The pride of life tempts us to get all the attention and glory for ourselves.

Satan tempted both Adam and Jesus through each of these three channels. Adam failed in a big way, and we still suffer the results of his failure and fall. But Jesus Christ met Satan's three-level temptation head on and succeeded triumphantly. In Him we have the example and the power to conquer every temptation Satan throws at us.

The Lust of the Flesh

Satan first approached Eve through the channel of the lust of the flesh. He planted a doubt in her mind about the fruit of the tree when he said: "Has God said, 'You shall not eat from any tree of the garden'?" (Genesis 3:1). Actually, God didn't say, "any tree," only the one tree. Satan distorts the Word of God. Eve answered, "God has said, 'You shall not eat from it or touch it' " (verse 3). Eve also distorted God's Word when she added, "or touch it." But Satan had aroused her appetite for the forbidden fruit, and she "saw that the tree was good for food" (verse 6) and ate some of it. Yielding to the lust of the flesh contributed to Adam and Eve's downfall.

Satan also challenged Jesus through the channel of the lust of the flesh. Our Lord had been fasting (going without food) for 40 days when Satan tempted Him through the weak point of his hunger: "If You are the Son of God, command that these stones become bread" (Matthew 4:3).

Satan doesn't know everything, but he's not blind either. He learned that Jesus was hungry by watching Him go without food for 40 days. He's watching us too, looking for soft spots and weaknesses in our physical appetites for food, rest, comfort, and sex. Temptation is greatest when we are especially hungry, tired, or lonely.

The temptation of the lust of the flesh is designed to draw us away from the will of God to please ourselves (Galatians 5:16,17). There is nothing sinful about eating. Eating is a physical need, and God created food so we could meet that need. But about that one fruit in the garden, God said to Adam and Eve, "Don't eat it." By eating, Adam and Eve went against God's will.

In the same way, there was nothing wrong with Jesus eating bread at the end of His fast, except that it wasn't the Father's will for Him to do so yet. Jesus replied: "Man shall not live on bread alone, but on every word that proceeds out of the mouth of God" (Matthew 4:4). No matter how desirable a loaf of bread seemed to Jesus in His hunger, He was not about to act outside of the Father's will by accepting Satan's offer. The life that Jesus modeled was a life totally dependent on God the Father (John 5:30; 6:57; 8:42; 14:10; 17:7). All temptation is an attempt by Satan to get us to live our lives independently of God.

When Satan tempts us through the channel of the lust of the flesh, he will invite us to meet our physical needs in ways that are outside the boundary of God's will. Eating is necessary and right, but eating too much, eating the wrong kinds of foods, and allowing food to rule our lives are wrong. God intended sex to be beautiful and good. But sex outside of marriage, homosexuality, and selfish sex are out-of-bounds and lead to bondage.

Whenever you feel enticed to meet a physical need by acting outside of God's will, you are being tempted through the lust of the flesh. When you resist the temptations of the lust of the flesh, you are declaring your dependence on God for your natural needs. (To learn more about God's design for sex, friendships, and freedom, read *Purity Under Pressure* by

Neil and Dave or check out the 40-day devotional *Ultimate Love*. Both books are published by Harvest House.)

The Lust of the Eyes

The second channel of temptation Satan used on Adam and Eve was based on a lie. Satan lied about what would happen if Adam and Eve disobeyed God. God had said that disobedience would lead to death, but Satan said, "You surely will not die!" (Genesis 3:4). "Don't listen to God. Do what *you* think is right," he urged Eve. The forbidden fruit was a delight to her eyes (verse 6), so she and Adam ignored God's command and did what they decided was best for them.

The lust of the eyes gradually draws us away from the Word of God and eats away at our confidence in God. We see what the world has to offer and desire those things more than our relationship with God. We begin to trust in our own view of life more than in God's commands and promises. We get excited about all the stuff we see around us and grab for all we can get. We convince ourselves that we need it and that God wants us to have it.

Instead of trusting God wholeheartedly, we adopt a "prove it to me" attitude. That's what Satan's second temptation of Jesus was all about: "If You are the Son of God, throw Yourself down [from the top of the temple]; for it is written, 'He will command His angels concerning You'; and 'On their hands they will bear You up, so that You will not strike Your foot against a stone'" (Matthew 4:6).

But Jesus wasn't about to play Satan's "show me" game. He replied, "It is written, 'You shall not put the Lord your God to the test'" (verse 7).

When you resist the temptations of the lust of the eyes, you are choosing to follow the Word of God instead of your own idea of how to run your life. The righteous shall live by faith in the written Word of God and not demand that God prove Himself by fulfilling their wishes, no matter how noble they are.

The Pride of Life

The third channel of temptation is at the heart of the New Age movement: the temptation to direct our own future, to rule our own world, to be our own god. Satan tempted Eve with the forbidden fruit: "The day you eat from it your eyes will be opened, and you will be like God, knowing good and evil" (Genesis 3:5). Satan's offer was an appeal to the ability God gave us to rule. "Don't be satisfied ruling *under* God," he seemed to say, "when you have the potential to *be* God." When Eve was convinced that "the tree was desirable to make one wise" (verse 6), she and Adam ate.

Satan's promise that the couple would become like God was nothing more than a lie. When Adam and Eve yielded to his temptation, they didn't become the gods of this world as he claimed they would. Instead, they fell from their position of rulership with God, and Satan became the god of this world—exactly as he had planned.

Satan tried the same trick on Jesus: "The devil took Him to a very high mountain, and showed Him all the kingdoms of the world and their glory; and he said to Him, 'All these things I will give You, if You fall down and worship me'" (Matthew 4:8,9). Satan was the god of this world, so the kingdoms of the world were his to offer to Jesus.

When you think about it, however, Satan's offer was pretty ridiculous. Why would Jesus be tempted to worship Satan in exchange for the world when He already owned the universe? So He replied, "Go, Satan! For it is written, 'You shall worship the Lord your God, and serve Him only'" (verse 10).

The temptation of the pride of life is intended to steer you away from the worship of God and destroy your obedience to

God by urging you to take charge of your own life. Whenever you feel that you don't need God's help or direction, that you can handle your life without going to Him, that you don't need to submit to anyone, beware: That's the pride of life.

You may think you are serving yourself, but whenever you stop worshiping and serving God you are really worshiping and serving Satan—which is what he wants more than anything else. Instead, your life should be marked by worshipful humility and obedience to God (1 Peter 5:5-11; John 15:8-10).

Remember, there are three critical issues reflected in these channels of temptation: 1) the *will of God* in your life, seen through your dependence on God; 2) the *Word of God* in your life, seen through your confidence in God; and 3) the *worship of God* in your life, seen through your obedience to God. Every temptation that Satan throws at you will challenge one or more of these issues. He will watch you to learn where you are weak and will tempt you in any area that you leave unguarded.

Why do we entertain tempting thoughts that are contrary to God's Word and God's will? Let's face it—we want to. We're not tempted to overeat foods we don't like, to think impure thoughts about unattractive guys or girls, or to shoplift something we don't want. The devil's hook is his guarantee that what we think we want and need outside God's will can satisfy us. Don't believe it. You can never satisfy the desires of the flesh. Instead, "Blessed are those who hunger and thirst for righteousness, for they shall be satisfied" (Matthew 5:6). Only right relationships, living by the power of the Holy Spirit, and experiencing the fruit of the Spirit will satisfy you.

The Way of Escape

First Corinthians 10:13 is the shining good news in the midst of our fears and concerns about temptation: "No temptation has overtaken you but such as is common to man; and God is faithful, who will not allow you to be tempted beyond what you are able, but with the temptation will provide the way of escape also, so that you will be able to endure it."

Where is the escape hatch that Paul is talking about here? In the same place where temptation starts: in our mind. Every temptation begins as a thought introduced to our mind by our own evil desires or the devil himself. If we hold that thought and consider acting it out, we will eventually do it, and that's sin. Instead Paul tells us to take every thought captive to the obedience of Christ (2 Corinthians 10:5). The first step for escaping temptation is to capture every thought as soon as it steps through the doorway of your mind.

Once you have halted an incoming thought, the next step is to check it out to see if it passes the eight-part test based on Philippians 4:8 for what we should think about:

1. Does this thought line up with God's truth?
2. Does it suggest that I do something honorable?
3. Is it right?
4. Is it pure?
5. Will the outcome of this thought be lovely?
6. Will the result be something to admire?
7. Will it contribute to excellence in my life?
8. Is it something for which I can praise God?

If the answer to any of these questions is no, kick the thought out immediately. Don't have anything more to do with it. If it keeps coming back, keep saying no. When you learn to respond to tempting thoughts by stopping them at the door of your mind, evaluating them on the basis of God's Word, and dismissing those which fail the test, you have found the way of escape that God's Word promises.

On the other hand, if a thought comes into your mind and it passes the Philippians 4:8 test of truth, honor, righteousness, and so on, "let your mind dwell on these things" (verse 8) and "practice these things" (verse 9). "And the God of peace will be with you" (verse 9), which is a much better result than the pain and stress that follow when we yield to tempting thoughts and become involved in sinful behavior.

Submit, Confess, Resist, and Repent

"But sometimes I yield to temptation and sin," some Christians complain. "I confess my sin, but when I'm tempted again, I sin again. It seems like I'm riding a roller coaster of ups and downs—sin, confess, sin, confess, sin, confess—and I can't get off."

People who are caught in the sin-confess cycle eventually begin to lose hope that they can experience any real victory over sin. Sheer willpower can't keep them from repeating the sin they just confessed, and Satan pours on the guilt.

Sin that is allowed to reign is like a dog that gets into your yard, bites you on the leg, and won't let go. First you're tempted from the other side of the fence: "Come on. Everyone else does it. Open the gate—you'll get away with it." But when you give in to the temptation, the tune changes: "You opened the gate! You opened the gate!" The tempter changes roles and becomes the accuser. You beat on yourself for your failure and cry out to God for forgiveness. He has already forgiven you, but the dog is still there.

Why not cry out to God and beat on the dog instead of on yourself? James 4:7 tells us, "Submit therefore to God. Resist the devil and he will flee from you." We must confess our sin, but there are two more important steps that break the cycle: sin-confess-*resist-repent*. Once the dog is gone, close the door. If you don't change, the same thing will happen again.

The apostle John wrote: "My little children, I am writing these things to you so that you may not sin. And if anyone sins, we have an Advocate [defender] with the Father, Jesus Christ the righteous" (1 John 2:1). We must turn to our righteous defender, resist our adversary, and *change* if we are to experience victory and freedom over temptation and sin.

Truth Encounter

Read:

1 Corinthians 10:13; James 4:7; 2 Corinthians 10:5;
Philippians 4:8

Reflect:

1. What are some common ways that Satan and his demons try to tempt us in the area of our physical appetites?

2. What are some common ways that we are tempted to trust in ourselves and our own knowledge rather than in God and His Word?

3. What does it mean to take every thought captive?

4. What does Philippians 4:8 ask us to think through in relation to taking thoughts captive? Can you name some of the eight steps talked about in the verse?

5. Jesus is defending you before the Father from Satan's accusations (1 John 2:1). How does knowing this help you stand strong against Satan's accusations?

Respond:

Read Philippians 4:8 once again. Now think of an issue you're struggling with in your life and imagine the possible choices you have. Pray and ask God to reveal to you whether your choices line up with His Word. Are they honorable, right, and pure? Will they please God?

Accused by the Father of Lies

TEN

WHEN I (DAVE) WAS IN JUNIOR HIGH, I was a wrestler. I remember the tournament in which I competed for the championship. I had wrestled all day and had won every match. Now I would face my toughest opponent. He would have to be a good wrestler to make it to the final round. But I was pumped. I felt like I could beat anybody.

When I saw the boy I was going to wrestle for the championship, my heart sank. It was my coach's son. The coach stood silently at the edge of the mat. But I knew he wanted his son to win. What father wouldn't? It was like I was going for the championship without a coach. My mind filled with doubts. I began to question my abilities. Phrases like, "I'm not good enough" and "I can't beat him," rattled through my mind. I soon convinced myself that there was no way I could ever beat the coach's son.

Well, I lost. But I can't say that my opponent's wrestling skills defeated me that day. I had lost the match before I even stepped onto the mat by believing the doubts in my mind.

Teenagers seem to have one sad thing in common: All kids are pretty good at putting themselves down like I did that day. They say, "I'm not important, I'm not qualified, I'm no good." It's amazing how many young Christians are paralyzed in their witness and growth because they think and feel they are worthless.

This discouraging inner criticism may have its roots in the kingdom of darkness. Next to temptation, perhaps the most frequent and insistent attack Satan throws at us is *accusation*. In Christ we *are* important, we *are* qualified, we *are* good. Satan can do nothing to change our position in Christ and our worth to God. But he can defeat us if he can trick us into believing his lies that we are of little value to God or other people.

Satan's two favorite moves are temptation and accusation. He uses them to pin us down and defeat us. He comes along and says, "Why don't you try it? Everybody does it. Besides, you can get away with it. Who's going to know?" Then as soon as we fall for his tempting line, he changes his tune to accusation: "What kind of a Christian are you to do such a thing? You're a sad excuse for a child of God. You'll never get away with it. You might as well give up because God has already given up on you."

Satan is called "the accuser of our brothers…who accuses them before our God day and night" (Revelation 12:10 NIV). We have all heard his lying, hateful voice in our hearts and minds. He never seems to let up on us. Many Christians are always discouraged and defeated because they believe his lies about them. And those who give in to his accusations end up being robbed of the freedom that God intends His people to enjoy. One defeated Christian wrote:

> My old feelings that life isn't worth the trouble keep coming back. I'm scared, lonely, confused, and very desperate. I know deep down that God can overcome this, but I can't get past this block. I can't even pray. When I try, things get in my way. When I'm feeling good and I begin putting into action what I know God wants me to

do, I'm stopped dead in my tracks by those voices and a force so strong I can't continue. I'm so close to giving in to those voices that I almost can't fight them anymore. I just want some peace.

Putting the Accuser in His Place

The good news is that we don't have to listen to Satan's accusations and live in defeat. Zechariah 3:1-10 contains an important truth we need to grab hold of in order to stand by faith against Satan's accusations and to live righteously in the service of God.

The Lord showed the prophet Zechariah a heavenly scene in which Satan's accusations of God's people are put into proper perspective:

> Then he showed me Joshua the high priest standing before the angel of the LORD, and Satan standing at his right hand to accuse him. The LORD said to Satan, "The LORD rebuke you, Satan! Indeed, the LORD who has chosen Jerusalem rebuke you! Is this not a brand plucked from the fire?" Now Joshua was clothed with filthy garments and standing before the angel (verses 1-3).

The Lord Rebukes Satan

Look at the cast of characters in this scene. It looks like a heavenly courtroom. The judge is God the Father. The prosecuting attorney is Satan. The defense attorney is Jesus. And the accused defendant is Joshua the high priest, who represents all of God's people, including you and me.

In Hebrew history, when the high priest entered God's presence in the holy of holies (the place where the sacrifice for sin was offered) once a year, it was a very serious occasion. The priest had to perform special ceremonies to make sure he was clean before God. If the priest wasn't just right before God, he could be struck dead on the spot. The priest wore bells on the hem of his robe so the priests outside the holy of holies could tell if he was still alive and moving. They even tied a rope around his ankle so he could be dragged out if he dropped dead in God's presence.

So here is a high priest named Joshua, standing in God's presence with filthy garments representing the sins of Israel. Bad news! Satan the accuser says, "Look at him, God. He's filthy. He deserves to be struck dead." But God rebukes the accuser and puts him in his place. "You're not the judge, and you cannot pass sentence on My people," God seems to say in His rebuke. "I have rescued Joshua from the flames of judgment, and your accusations are false."

This courtroom scene is going on night and day for every child of God. Satan keeps pointing out our faults and weaknesses to God and demands that He zap us for being less than perfect. But our defense attorney in heaven is Jesus Christ, and He has never lost a case before God the judge. Satan can't make his accusations stick because Jesus Christ took our sins upon Himself at the cross. He has made us right with God and stands before God in our defense (Romans 8:33,34).

While Satan accuses us before God, he and his demons also accuse us by bombarding our minds with false thoughts of how unworthy and unrighteous we are in God's sight: "How could you do that and be a Christian? You're not really a child of God." But Satan is not our judge; he is only our *accuser*. Yet if we listen to him and believe him, we will begin to live out these accusations as if they were a sentence we must serve.

When Satan's accusations of unworthiness attack you, don't pay attention to them. Instead respond, "Satan, I have put my trust in Christ, and I am a child of God. Like Joshua the high priest, I have been rescued by God from the fire of judgment. He has declared me righteous. You're not the judge. All you can do is accuse me—and I don't buy it."

The Lord Removes Our Filthy Garments

The reason Satan's accusations are false is because God has solved the problem of our filthy garments, meaning our sin. Zechariah's description of the heavenly courtroom scene continues:

> He spoke and said to those who were standing before him, saying, "Remove the filthy garments from him." Again he said to him, "See, I have taken your iniquity away from you and will clothe you with festal robes." Then I said, "Let them put a clean turban on his head." So they put a clean turban on his head and clothed him with garments, while the angel of the LORD was standing by (3:4,5).

God has not only declared us righteous, but He has removed our filthy garments of sin and clothed us with His righteousness. Notice that the change of wardrobe is something that *God* does, not us. In ourselves, we don't have any garments of righteousness to put on that will satisfy God. He changes us when we give our lives to Him in faith.

The Lord Asks Us to Respond

Having rebuked Satan and provided our righteousness, the Lord calls us to respond with obedience: "If you will walk in My ways and if you will perform My service, then you will also govern My house and also have charge of My courts, and I will grant you free access among these who are standing here" (Zechariah 3:7).

In calling us to walk in His ways and perform His service, the Lord is simply calling us to live out our identity in Christ through our obedience. This means living by faith instead of fear. It means crucifying the flesh on a daily basis and walking according to the Spirit. It means believing that we are dead to sin and alive to God and not allowing sin to rule in our bodies. It means taking every thought captive to the obedience of Christ and being transformed by the renewing of our minds.

If we walk in obedience, God promises that we will govern His house and have charge of His courts. This means that we will actively experience our sharing in His authority in the spiritual world, able to live victoriously over Satan and sin. He also promises us an open line of communication with the Father. As we operate in His authority and live in fellowship and harmony with Him, our daily victory and fruitfulness are assured.

What's the Difference?

You may be thinking, "When the devil throws his accusations at me, I feel bummed out. But sometimes the Holy Spirit's conviction bums me out too. How can I tell the difference between Satan's accusations and the Spirit's conviction?"

Paul shows us the difference between the two in 2 Corinthians 7:9,10:

> I now rejoice, not that you were made sorrowful, but that you were made sorrowful to the point of repentance; for you were made

> sorrowful according to the will of God, so that
> you might not suffer loss in anything through
> us. For the sorrow that is according to the will
> of God produces a repentance without regret,
> leading to salvation, but the sorrow of the
> world produces death.

The devil's accusations and the Holy Spirit's conviction both bring feelings of sorrow. But the sorrow from Satan's accusations leads to death. In other words, the devil wants us to feel bad in order to destroy us. He wants us to give up and quit following Christ.

In contrast, the sorrow of conviction is allowed by God to prompt us to repent, which leads to life. God isn't beating us into the ground with sorrow. He wants our feelings of sorrow over our sin to bring us to Him so we can experience forgiveness and freedom.

Every young Christian is faced daily with the choice of walking by the Spirit or by the flesh. When we choose to walk according to the flesh, the Holy Spirit brings conviction because we are not acting in harmony with who we really are. If we continue in the flesh, we will feel the sorrow of conviction.

"How do I know which kind of sorrow I'm experiencing?" you may ask. "They feel the same." Figure out whether your feelings reflect the truth or a lie, and you will identify their source. Do you feel guilty, worthless, or stupid? That's a sorrow caused by accusation, because those feelings don't reflect truth. You are no longer guilty; you have been forgiven through your faith in Christ. You are not worthless; Jesus gave His life for you. You are not stupid; you can do all things through Christ.

When you find lies lurking beneath your feelings of sorrow—especially if your feelings keep pounding you into the ground—you are being falsely accused. Even if you were to change, you wouldn't feel any better, because Satan would then find something else to bug you about. To get rid of the sorrow of accusation, you must submit yourself to God and resist the devil and his lies.

But if you feel bummed out because you're not living the way God wants you to live, it's the Holy Spirit calling you to admit on the basis of 1 John 1:9, "Dear Lord, I was wrong." As soon as you confess and repent, God says, "I'm glad you shared that with Me. You're cleansed; now get on with life." And you walk away free. The sorrow is gone, and you have a new determination to obey God in the area of your failure.

The difference between accusation and conviction is clearly seen in the lives of two of Jesus' disciples: Judas and Peter. Judas was a thief and he allowed Satan to deceive him into betraying Jesus for 30 pieces of silver (Luke 22:3-5). When Judas came under the sorrow of the world, he hanged himself. Was his suicide the result of Satan's accusation or of God's conviction? It had to be accusation because it drove Judas to kill himself. Accusation leads to death; conviction leads to repentance and life.

Peter also failed Jesus by denying Him (Luke 22:33,34). The sorrow Peter felt was every bit as painful as that which Judas experienced. But Peter's sorrow was from conviction that eventually led him to repent (John 21:15-17).

When your feelings of sorrow pound you into the ground and drive you from God, you are being accused by Satan. Resist it. But when your sorrow draws you to Christ to confess your wrong, you are being convicted by the Spirit. Yield to it and repent.

According to Revelation 12:10, Satan's continuing work is to accuse God's children. But Christ's continuing work is to pray for us (Hebrews 7:25). We have a persistent enemy, but we have an even more persistent, eternal Savior who defends us before the Father on the basis of our faith in Him (1 John 2:1).

The Quicksand of Accusation

It is very important to our daily victory in Christ that we learn to resist the accusations of Satan. We have all felt like worthless nobodies at times. When we feel like worthless nobodies, we act like worthless nobodies, and our lives suffer until we resist Satan and return to a life of victory.

But Satan never gives up. He will try to get us down more often and keep us down longer by firing one false accusation after another at us. If we fail to keep resisting him, we may become targets for even more serious attacks from Satan.

The Unpardonable Sin

One of the most serious accusations Satan throws at us is that we've committed "the unpardonable sin"—blaspheming the Holy Spirit. It's critical to untangle the devil's lies about this. Otherwise we can suffer in silence, with our helmet of salvation (Ephesians 6:17) seeming to do us no good because we're believing a lie about who we are.

This accusation is typical of the enemy's lying ways. He loves to twist and misuse the Scriptures, hoping to fool us into thinking that the Bible is condemning us. So it's important to look at and understand the *truth* of God's Word. Here's what Jesus said in Mark 3:22-30 (NIV):

The teachers of the law who came down from Jerusalem said, "He is possessed by Beelzebub! By the prince of demons he is driving out demons."

Jesus called them and spoke to them in parables: "How can Satan drive out Satan?…If a house is divided against itself, that house cannot stand. And if Satan opposes himself and is divided, he cannot stand.…I tell you the truth, all the sins and blasphemies of men will be forgiven them. But whoever blasphemes against the Holy Spirit will never be forgiven; he is guilty of an eternal sin."

He said this because they were saying, "He has an evil spirit."

It's the job of the Holy Spirit to bring people to Jesus. If you reject what the Spirit says about Him, then you can never come to Christ and salvation. You'll simply never come to Jesus in the first place. But if you do come to Him, God makes you His child and *all* of your sins and blasphemies are forgiven because of Jesus. This is why no Christian can commit the unpardonable sin.

Picture the scribes and Pharisees. Standing in front of them was their Messiah, Jesus, the Son of God—and they were accusing him of using Satan's power to free people from demonic bondage! They totally rejected what God's Spirit was telling them. Then later on, they were the ones who conspired to have him arrested and killed. They cursed Him and jeered at Him while He hung on the cross.

If you've been convicted by the Holy Spirit and have trusted in Christ, you've done the *opposite* of committing the unpardonable sin. If you feel convicted about your sins, that's more proof that you're a Christian. You wouldn't even be bothered about your sin if the Spirit weren't at work inside you!

You may be flat on your face because of Satan's deception in this area. Choose to believe God's truth. Submit yourself to Him, resist the devil, get up, and walk free.

Remember Who Our Enemy Is

Trying to make us think we've committed the unpardonable sin is just one of Satan's strategies. Remember that the devil is an accuser who will come at us any way he can. He's like a prosecuting attorney who's trying to smear and harass a witness with his lies. He points his slimy finger at us and says, "Aha! Now you've done it! This time you've gone over the line!"

What can happen to a Christian who fails to take a stand against Satan the accuser in his or her life? Janelle's story is an extreme case, but it shows how important it is to choose the truth over the evil one's deception.

Janelle was a young Christian with severe emotional problems who was brought to me (Neil) by her elderly pastor. Janelle's fiancé, Curt, came with them. After introducing me to Janelle and Curt, the pastor started to leave. "Wait a minute," I said. "I'd prefer that you stay with us."

"I've got a bad heart," the pastor replied.

"I don't think anything will happen here today that will affect your heart," I assured him. (I had no idea what was about to happen!) "Besides, you're her pastor, and I would appreciate your prayer support." He reluctantly agreed.

As Janelle told me her story, I realized that Satan the accuser had really done a number on her. She had been the victim of one abuse after another as a child and teenager. Her background also included a sick relationship with a previous boyfriend who was involved in the occult. Over the years she had come to believe Satan's lies that she was the cause of her troubles and that she was of no value to God or anybody else. Her view of herself was down in the mud.

Recognizing Satan's familiar strategy, I said, "Janelle, we can help you with your problems because there is a battle going on for your mind that God has given us the authority to win." As soon as I spoke those words, Janelle suddenly went blank. She sat as still as a stone, eyes glazed over and staring into space.

"Have you ever seen her behave like this?" I asked her pastor and fiancé.

"No," they answered, wide-eyed. They were really frightened.

"Well, there's nothing to worry about. I've seen it before," I said. "We're going to take authority over it, but it's important that you two affirm your right standing with God."

I led the pastor in a prayer similar to those found in Chapter 13 of this book. When I turned to lead Curt in prayer, he started to shake.

"Curt, is there something between you and God that's not right? If so, I suggest you get it cleared up right now."

Under the circumstances, Curt didn't need much prompting! He began confessing sin in his life, including the fact that he and Janelle had been sleeping together. I counseled Curt to end that practice, and he said he would. All the while Janelle sat motionless, totally blanked out.

After we had prayed together about getting his life straight with God, I gave Curt a sheet of paper with a prayer on it to read. As soon as Curt began reading the prayer, Janelle snapped to life. She let out a growl, then lashed out and slapped the paper out of Curt's hands. Satan tried to use the suddenness of her actions to frighten us, and for an instant I was startled. But it was just another of his tactics designed to make us shrink back in fear. We exercised God's authority and agreed in prayer that the evil one be bound in the name of the Lord Jesus Christ.

I wish I could have videotaped Janelle that day in order to show skeptics what happens when Satan is confronted by God's authority. It was as if Wonder Woman had tied Janelle to the chair. She just sat there squirming, bound by the ropes of God's authority. Her eyes blazed at Curt with hatred, which was further evidence of the demonic power which was controlling her. Janelle didn't hate Curt; she loved him. They were going to be married. But Satan hated the fact that his strongholds in Curt and Janelle were being torn down, and his hatred was displayed on Janelle's face.

Curt finished reading the prayer while Janelle continued to squirm in her chair. Then I prayed, "Lord, we declare our dependence on You, for apart from Christ we can do nothing. Now, in the name and authority of the Lord Jesus Christ, we command Satan and all his forces to release Janelle and to remain bound so she will be free to obey God her heavenly Father."

Suddenly Janelle slumped in her chair and snapped out of her trance.

"Do you remember anything we've been doing here?" I asked her.

"No, what happened?" she responded with a puzzled look.

"It's nothing to worry about," I told her. "Somehow Satan has gained a foothold in your life. But we would like to walk you through the Steps to Freedom in Christ." About an hour later Janelle was free.

What right did Satan have to control Janelle as he did? Only the right she gave him by yielding to his lies. Satan had convinced her that she was practically worthless. So she lived on the fringe of immorality and dabbled in the occult, which gave Satan even more room to work in her life and partially control her. But once Janelle renounced her involvement with sin and Satan, his hold on her was canceled, and he had to leave.

For most of us, Satan's deceptive accusations will not result in the kind of bondage seen in Janelle's life. But if he can cause you to doubt your worth to God or your effectiveness as God's child through his accusations, he can stop you from living for God. Put your feelings to the test. Take every thought captive. Don't believe anything Satan says about you; it's a lie. Believe everything God says about you; it's the truth that will set you free.

Truth Encounter

Read:
Zechariah 3:1-7

Reflect:

1. What is an accusation? Does God ever condemn or accuse us? What is the difference between accusation and conviction?

2. What are some of the accusations Satan uses to tear down believers today? Why is it sometimes hard to ignore those accusations?

3. Why do we sometimes try to earn God's love and acceptance even though we already have it? Why is it hard to think of ourselves as righteous even though God says we are?

4. Why can't you as a Christian commit the "unpardonable sin"?

5. When you feel you are being accused by the enemy, how should you respond? In what ways do you need to act differently when it comes to handling accusation?

Respond:

Pray and proclaim to God who you are in Christ. Thank Him that there is now no punishment for those who are in Christ and that Satan isn't able to bring any charges against us that the blood of Christ hasn't taken away.

The Danger of Deception

ELEVEN

ALYCE WAS ONE OF THE MOST pathetic-looking young women I (Neil) have ever met. She was skinny and had no more body fat to lose. Her sad, empty eyes told me that she had lost all hope for her life.

Alyce's father said that she was addicted to prescription painkillers. She was a very talented girl and a committed Christian in many respects, but she was also a Darvon junkie who had even been arrested once for illegal possession of prescription drugs. As her father told me her sad story, Alyce sat nodding to herself as if to say, "Yes, that's me, and life is the pits."

Finally I turned to Alyce, took her by the hands, and said, "I want you to tell me who you think you are."

"I'm just a no-good failure," she whimpered.

"You're not a failure," I responded. "You're a child of God." She continued to pour out the negative self-talk, which indicated to me that she had been living under demonic deception. I continued to remind her of the good news of her identity in Christ. The more we talked, the more aware I became of Christ's presence ministering to Alyce.

Finally she said, "Do you mean to tell me that all these negative thoughts about myself are nothing but Satan's lies?"

"That's right, Alyce," I nodded. "And as you begin to learn the truth about your identity in Christ, you will be free from the bondage of Satan's lies."

Two weeks later Alyce was enrolled in an intensive 12-week spiritual growth course. At the end of the course, she began to take control of her life instead of remaining the victim of Satan's deception. She gained about 25 pounds. And today she's free.

The main theme of the New Testament is the position we enjoy in Christ through our faith in Him. That's the good news: Christ in you and you in Christ. If there is a negative theme in the New Testament that sums up the opposition we face from Satan, it would be *deception*.

There are three main things that Satan will use to try to steer you away from God's truth and deceive you into believing his lies: self-deception, false prophets and teachers, and deceiving spirits. We are the targets for Satan's deception in these areas if we fail to fill our minds with the truth of God's Word.

Beware of Self-Deception

Is it really possible for Christians to deceive themselves? Yes, it is very possible. The Bible tells us about several ways that we as Christians deceive ourselves.

We deceive ourselves when we hear the Word but don't do it (James 1:22; 1 Peter 1:13). We hear the pastor's sermon or the youth leader's Bible study lesson and say, "Wow! What a great truth!" Then we hurry off to share it with someone else, without thinking how it applies to our own lives. James said people who hear the Word but don't do what it says deceive themselves (1:22).

We deceive ourselves when we say we have no sin (1 John 1:8). The Bible doesn't say that we *are* sin; it says that it is possible for us to sin and for sin to reside in our bodies (Romans 6:12). We are not sinless saints; we are saints who sometimes sin. It's important to recognize our failures, confess them to God, and receive His forgiveness. The person who deceives himself by ignoring his sinful acts and allowing them to build up is headed for a great fall.

People who live in earthquake-prone southern California keep hearing about "the big one" that many experts think is coming. Whenever they experience minor earthquakes, they may be frightened by them a bit, but they also see them as a good sign. These little shakes mean that the plates in the earth's crust are shifting. As long as the crust is adjusting in this way, it's unlikely that "the big one" will hit. But when no minor earthquakes happen for several months or years, the danger of a major, devastating quake increases.

When we live in obedience to God's Word and deal with our sin on a daily basis, we prevent the major spiritual earthquakes from building up in our lives. If we keep saying, "I don't have any sin," or if we fail to admit our failures as God convicts us of them, we're in for "the big one."

We deceive ourselves when we think we are better than we are (Romans 12:3; Galatians 6:3). "But I know who I am," we say. "I'm a child of God, I'm seated with Christ, I can do all things through Him. That makes me pretty special." Yes, we are very special in the eyes of God. But we are what we are by the grace of God (1 Corinthians 15:10). The life we live, the talents we possess, and the gifts we have received are not personal accomplishments; they are expressions of God's grace. We must never take credit for what God has provided. Rather, we must find joy in doing things that glorify the Lord.

We deceive ourselves when we think we are smarter than we are (1 Corinthians 3:18,19). Sometimes we are tempted to think we are as smart as Satan, the god of this world. But we are no match for him. Whenever we think we can outsmart Satan on our own, we become a prime target to be hit by one of his crafty tricks.

However, Satan is no match for God. It is important for us not to lean on our own understanding, but to use the mind of Christ and put Him first in all our ways (Proverbs 3:5,6; 1 Corinthians 2:16).

We deceive ourselves when we think we are good Christians but do not control our speech (James 1:26). There is nothing that saddens God more than when we bad-mouth others instead of building them up with our speech. We are never to use our tongues to put others down. Instead, we are to build each other up in what we say. If our speech is out of control, we're fooling ourselves to believe that we have our spiritual life together.

We deceive ourselves when we think our sin will not lead to consequences (Galatians 6:7). As Christians we sometimes think we have special privileges—that our sins won't have any bad effects. But we have to live with the results and consequences of our thoughts, words, and actions, just like unbelievers.

We deceive ourselves when we think people living totally in sin are Christians (1 Corinthians 6:9,10). Kate, a co-worker of mine (Neil), walked into the office one day completely devastated. She had just learned that her older sister, who had led her to Christ, had walked away from God and was living in a lesbian relationship. "My lifestyle doesn't make any difference," Kate's sister had argued. "God loves me and I'm forgiven." Kate was distraught and confused.

I showed her 1 Corinthians 6:9,10: "Don't fool yourselves. Those who live immoral lives, who are idol worshipers, adulterers or homosexuals—will have no share in [God's] kingdom" (TLB). Kate's sister and others like her are deceived. Living a consistently sinful life is strong evidence that a person is not in right relationship with God. We are absolutely deceived if we believe that our walk doesn't have to line up with our talk.

We deceive ourselves when we think we can always hang out with bad people and not be influenced by them (1 Corinthians 15:33). My (Dave's) brother-in-law was raised in a strong and loving Christian home, so he thought he could hang out with ungodly people and not be affected. But he was enticed so far from his values that he actually became part of a vicious hate group called the skinheads.

Does this mean that we shouldn't minister to those with bad morals? No, we must share Christ with them. But if we spend all our time on their turf, our ministry will eventually dry up, and our morality will be affected for the worse.

Beware of False Prophets and Teachers

Alvin was discouraged and defeated. He came to see me (Neil) because for several years he had believed he had a special gift of prophecy from God. But over a period of months, his personal life began to fall apart. Alvin eventually reached the point where he began to withdraw from people completely. He was a slave to prescription drugs and had checked out of society.

Alvin and I read 1 Thessalonians 5:19-21: "Do not put out the Spirit's fire; do not treat prophecies with contempt. Test everything. Hold on to the good" (NIV). I said, "Alvin, I'm not against prophecy; it's a spiritual gift. But Satan can produce fake spiritual gifts and deceive us into believing they're from God. That's why the Scriptures instruct us to put everything to the test."

After a lengthy discussion about false prophets and teachers, Alvin admitted, "I think my problems began when I failed to test the 'gifts' of tongues and prophecy given to me by false teachers. Not only was I deceived, but I have deceived others myself."

"Would you be willing to put your gift of tongues to the test?" I asked. I assured Alvin that I was interested in testing the spirit, not him.

Alvin really wanted to be free of deception and right with God. "Yes," he answered.

I asked Alvin to begin praying aloud in his "spiritual language." As he began to chant in a language I couldn't understand, I said, "In the name of Christ and in obedience to God's Word, I command you, spirit, to identify yourself."

Alvin stopped in the middle of his chanting and said, "I am he."

"Are you the 'he' who was crucified, buried, raised on the third day, and who now sits at the right hand of the Father?" I continued.

Alvin almost shouted the response: "No! Not he!" I led Alvin through a prayer renouncing Satan's activity in his life, and he was free from that deception.

We're not against spiritual gifts, even prophecy and tongues. We are, however, committed to obeying Scripture. First Corinthians 14:39 says, "Desire earnestly to prophesy, and do not forbid to speak in tongues." But Scripture also requires that all spiritual gifts be tested. False prophets and teachers are popular everywhere today simply because Christians accept their ministry without testing the spirits behind it.

Comparing the Phony with the Real

In Jeremiah 23, the Lord revealed through His prophet several qualifications for a true prophet from God.

A true prophet brings people to God (verses 16,21,22). Every true prophet of God in the Old Testament was an evangelist. The prophet's ministry drew people back to God and His Word. If you come across someone who claims to be a prophet, but who is not involved in calling people to a righteous walk with God, you may be dealing with a phony.

A true prophet's dreams agree with God's Word (verses 25,28). God often spoke to people in the Bible through the dreams of godly people. In these verses, God compares dreams to straw and His Word to grain. If you feed straw to cattle, they'll die. They will sleep on it, but they won't eat it because it has no nutrients. In the same way, dreams are of some value, but they are never to be made equal to God's Word as the basis for our faith or our walk. Dreams must be checked out against God's Word; it's never the other way around.

A true prophet's message moves people to get right with God (verse 29). Jeremiah writes: "'Is not my word like fire?' declares the LORD, 'and like a hammer which shatters a rock?'" If you attend a youth group meeting or church where prophecies are part of the worship service, don't expect sugar-sweet messages from God like, "I love you, My children" or "I'm coming soon." These statements are certainly true. But why would they need to be prophesied, since the Bible clearly teaches God's love and Christ's soon return?

The voice of a prophet should be like a consuming fire and a shattering hammer. A prophetic message should motivate people to righteousness, not leave them comfortable in their sin (1 Peter 4:17).

The true prophet gets his message from God, not from other people (verses 30,31). Taking what God gave someone else and using it as if it were your own is called plagiarism—stealing someone else's ideas. Also, declaring that what you are saying is directly from the Lord when it isn't is an incredible slam against God. Has anybody ever come up to you and said, "The Lord told me to tell you…"? You can respond, "No, I don't believe He did! If God wants me to know something, He can tell me directly."

God can and will encourage us and confirm His Word to us through other people. But when it comes to receiving direction for our life, "there is one God, and one mediator also between God and men, the man Christ Jesus" (1 Timothy 2:5). If someone says to you, "God told me to tell you…," that person may be acting as a spiritual medium. And listening to a medium is forbidden by the Bible.

Signs and Wonders: Who's Being Tested?

Many young Christians think that if a person can perform a miracle, he must be doing it with God's power. God can still use signs and wonders to show that His Word is true, but the Bible also warns that "there will be many false Messiahs and false prophets who will do wonderful miracles that would deceive, if possible, even God's own children" (Mark 13:22 TLB). Satan can also perform signs and wonders, but he only does so to direct our worship away from God to himself.

Deuteronomy 13:5-11 reveals the seriousness of attributing to God the activity of Satan. People who were involved in it were to be killed, even if they were relatives. We are to love God, obey His Word, and test all signs, wonders, and dreams.

Counterfeits in the Church

False prophets and false teachers are not just Eastern mystics and gurus and non-Christian cult leaders. The apostle

Peter devoted an entire chapter in one of his letters to false prophets and teachers who work *within* the church: "There will also be false teachers among you, who will secretly introduce destructive heresies, even denying the Master who bought them, bringing swift destruction upon themselves" (2 Peter 2:1). These people are in our churches right now, disguised as Christian leaders.

Notice that the attraction of false teachers is not primarily their doctrine: "Many will follow their sensuality" (verse 2). Peter is talking about Christians who evaluate a ministry based on the outward appearance and charm of its leaders. We say, "He's such a nice guy"; "She's a very charismatic person"; "He's a real dynamic speaker"; "She's so sweet and sounds so sincere."

But we are never to judge a ministry or its leaders on the basis of physical appearance or personality. The important issue is whether or not the person proclaims God's Word as the truth and calls people to get right with God through faith in Jesus Christ.

Peter goes on to reveal two ways we can identify false prophets and false teachers in the church. First, they will be involved in immorality of some kind (verse 10). They may be discovered in illegal and immoral activities involving sex or money or both. They may claim that God is full of love and grace, so we don't need to obey any moral laws. Their immorality may not be easy to spot, but it will eventually surface in their lives (2 Corinthians 11:15).

Second, false prophets and teachers "despise authority" and are "daring, self-willed" (2 Peter 2:10). These people do their own thing and won't answer to anybody. They either won't submit to the authority of those over them, or they will pick their own so-called leaders who will always agree with anything they want to do. Every true, committed Christian in a leadership role needs to submit himself and his ideas to other mature believers who will hold him accountable.

Beware of Deceiving Spirits

In addition to warning us against self-deception and false prophets and teachers, the Bible also warns us against the deception that comes through demonic influence. Paul alerted Timothy: "The Spirit explicitly says that in later times some will fall away from the faith, paying attention to deceitful spirits and doctrines of demons" (1 Timothy 4:1). John also cautioned us to test the spirits in order to know the difference between the spirit of truth and the spirit of error (1 John 4:1-6).

I (Dave) was reminded of the deception of evil spirits among young people when I talked to a girl named Ashley at a junior-high camp in Missouri. "I'm being visited by my dead sister, Brandy," she blurted out.

"Tell me what's happening," I said.

"After my sister died, my mother used to go visit Brandy's grave. Mom said Brandy would talk with her there for hours. Soon Mom said she could see Brandy, who rode part of the way home with her in the car. Eventually Brandy was visiting my mother at our home. Now even I can see her and talk to her."

I turned to Luke 16 in my Bible and asked Ashley to read aloud the story about the rich man and Lazarus (verses 19-26). Then I asked her to read verse 26 a second time, the verse that has the words of Abraham in heaven to the rich man in hell. Ashley read, "Between us and you there is a great chasm fixed, in order that those who wish to come over from here to you may not be able, and that none may cross over from there to us."

I said, "According to these verses, is the person visiting you and your mother really your sister?"

"No," she answered quickly, "it can't be, can it? No one can return from the dead."

"That's right, Ashley."

"But it looks and sounds exactly like her!"

"That's just part of Satan's deception. His demons are so evil and low that they will even impersonate a precious loved one to try to lead you away from God and His Word."

Ashley nodded. "I realize now that this thing is not my sister and it's not from God."

Although Ashley's experience is becoming more common among young people, it's more likely that Satan will try to influence our minds rather than appear to us. Satan's demonic forces are at work trying to pollute our minds with lies in order to keep us from walking in the truth.

The following is an example of the kind of prayer we need to pray in order to keep ourselves from deceiving spirits:

> *Heavenly Father, I commit myself totally to Your will. If I have been deceived in any way, I pray that You will open my eyes to the deception. I command in the name of the Lord Jesus Christ that all deceiving spirits depart from me. I reject all phony spiritual gifts or happenings. Lord, bless anything that is from You and cause it to grow so that Your body may be blessed and built up through it. Amen.*

Spiritual Discernment

Our first line of defense against Satan's deception is discernment. Discernment is that buzzer that sounds inside you, warning that something is wrong. Discernment simply means to make a judgment or a distinction. It has only one purpose: to distinguish right from wrong so the right can be encouraged and the wrong can be eliminated. In 1 Corinthians 12:10 discernment is the God-given ability to distinguish a good spirit from a bad spirit. It is one of the gifts of the Spirit that is to be used to build up the church.

Discernment is not an act of the mind; it's an act of the Holy Spirit, who dwells within us. When the Spirit sounds a warning, your mind, which is designed to deal with facts, may not be able to understand what's wrong. But when you discern that something is wrong, you don't need to understand it in order to act on the warning. Simply say to the people with you, "I sense that something is out of order here. Let's ask God to help us." Then allow God to bring the problem to light as only He can.

We are more vulnerable to Satan's deception than to any of his other schemes. Why? Because when he tempts us or accuses us, we know it. But when he *deceives* us, we *don't* know it. That's his strategy: to keep us in the dark. If he can get into our youth groups, our homes, and our minds without being noticed, he can control us with his lies. Sadly, he is doing just that across our land by deceiving many people.

You cannot expose Satan's deception by human reasoning; you can only do it by God's revelation. Jesus said, "If you continue in My word, then you are truly disciples of Mine; and you will know the truth, and the truth will make you free" (John 8:31,32). Jesus prayed, "Sanctify them [keep them from evil] in the truth; Your word is truth" (John 17:17).

When you put on the armor of God, it is important that you start with the belt of truth (Ephesians 6:14). The light of truth is the only valid weapon against the darkness of deception.

Here is an encouraging letter from a young girl who was trapped in deception until the Bondage Breaker set her free:

I will always remember the day I came to you for counsel and prayer. Ever since that day I have felt such freedom. There are no more voices or feelings of heaviness in my brain. I'm even enjoying a physical sense of release. Satan has returned many times trying to clobber me with those old thoughts, but his hold on me has been broken.

I'll never forget what you told me. You said that those negative thoughts about God and myself were lies that Satan planted in my mind. You said I have the power through Jesus Christ to rebuke Satan and get rid of the evil thoughts. It has taken me awhile to really believe that with all my heart, but lately I've decided to fight back—and it works! It's been wonderful to deal with my problems with a clear head. Thank you for helping me and so many others find peace and learn to trust, love, and believe in the Lord.

Love in Christ

Truth Encounter

Read:
James 4:7; Jeremiah 23:16-31

Reflect:

1. Do you have any Christian friends that seem to be defeated and deceived like the girl Alyce in this chapter? Is there hope for people who find themselves in bondage to Satan's lies? What is that hope?

2. In this chapter we talked a lot about self-deceptions. Which of these deceptions do you think is most common among Christian young people today? Which self-deception do you struggle with most?

3. What are some of the signs of a genuine prophet? Why should Christian leaders be accountable to other leaders in their ministry?

4. How can a false prophet be identified? Why is understanding God's Word so important when it comes to spotting a false prophet?

Respond:

Review the list of self-deceptions that are talked about in this chapter. Pray through each deception and ask God to reveal if you have knowingly or unknowingly become deceived in any of the areas talked about. Whatever God brings to mind, deal with it by first confessing the deception, then renouncing your involvement.

The Danger of
Losing Control

TWELVE

I RECEIVED THE FOLLOWING letter from a young woman I have never met. Sheila attended one of our conferences and wrote:

Dear Neil,

I have been set free—praise the Lord! Yesterday, for the first time in years, the voices stopped. I could hear the silence. When we sang, I could hear myself sing.

For the first 14 years of my life I lived with an oppressive, abusive mother who never said, "I love you," or put her arms around me when I cried. I received no affection, no kind words, no affirmation, no sense of who I was—only physical and emotional abuse. At 15 I was subjected to three weeks of Erhard Seminar Training (EST), which really screwed up my mind. The year which followed was pure hell. My mother threw me out, so I went to live with another family. Eventually they also threw me out.

Three years later I found Christ. My decision to trust Christ was largely based on my fear of

Satan and the power of evil I had experienced in my life. Even though I knew Satan had lost his ownership of me, I was unaware of how vulnerable I still was to his deception and control. For the first two years of my Christian life I was in bondage to a sin I didn't even know was a sin. Once I realized my sin, confessed it to God, and received forgiveness, I thought I was finally free of Satan's attempts to control me. I didn't realize that the battle had only begun.

I suffered from unexplainable rashes, hives, and welts all over my body. I lost my joy and closeness to the Lord. I could no longer sing or quote Scripture. I turned to food as my comfort and security. The demons attacked my sense of right and wrong, and I became involved in immorality in my search for identity and love.

But that all ended yesterday when I renounced Satan's control in my life. I have found the freedom and protection that comes from knowing I am loved. I'm not on a high. I'm writing with a clear mind, a clean spirit, and a calm hand. Even my previous bondage to food seems suddenly foreign to me.

I never realized that a Christian could be so vulnerable to Satan's control. I was deceived, but now I am free. Thank You, thank You, Jesus!

—Sheila

Sheila is a sobering example of a level of spiritual attack that most Christians don't like to talk about: demonic control. As a believer, Sheila had lost control in her eating habits, in her sexual behavior, and in her devotional life. She wasn't growing spiritually; she was shrinking. She didn't sing and read Scripture because she was blocked from doing so.

Most of us agree that Christians are clear targets for the enemy's temptation, accusation, and deception. But for some reason we hesitate to admit that Christians can lose control of their lives by surrendering to demonic influences. However, there is much clear evidence in Scripture that believers who repeatedly give in to temptation, accusation, and deception can lose their battle with sin and addiction.

Thankfully, demonic *bondage* does not mean satanic *ownership*. Like Sheila, we have been purchased by the blood of the Lamb, and not even the powers of hell can take our salvation away from us (1 Peter 1:17-19; Romans 8:35-39). Satan knows he can never own us again. But if he can deceive us into surrendering control of our life to him in some way, he can hinder our growth and our impact in the world for Christ. Since we live in a world whose god is Satan, the possibility of being tempted, deceived, and accused is continuous. If we allow his schemes to influence us, we can lose control to the degree that we have been deceived.

Saints in Bondage

It is very important that we understand that Christians are targets of demonic influence. Those who say a demon cannot affect a believer's life have left us with only two possible answers for the problems we face: Either we are the cause, or God is. If we blame ourselves, we feel hopeless because we can't do anything to stop what we're doing. If we blame God, our confidence in Him as our loving Father is shattered. Either way, we have no chance to gain the victory which the Bible promises us.

In reality, we are in a winnable war against demonic powers from the defeated kingdom of darkness. However, if Satan can get you to believe a lie, he can control your life.

Here are several indications from the Bible that believers can come under bondage to demonic influence.

Luke 13:10-17. While Jesus was teaching in the synagogue (the Jewish place of worship and study), "there was a woman who for eighteen years had had a sickness caused by a spirit; and she was bent double, and could not straighten up at all" (verse 11). Verse 16 states that her physical disability was caused by satanic bondage. This woman was not an unbeliever. She was a God-fearing woman of faith with a spiritual problem. As soon as Jesus released her from bondage, her physical problem was cured.

Notice that this woman wasn't protected from demonic control by being inside the synagogue. The walls of a church can't protect us from demonic influence either. If plaster walls are not a barrier to Satan, do you think your skin is? The spiritual world is not subject to such natural barriers.

Yes, this event occurred before the cross. But it is an indication that believers can be physically affected by demons.

Luke 22:31-34. The apostle Peter is an example of a believer who temporarily lost control to Satan. Jesus said to him, "Simon, Simon, behold, Satan has demanded permission to sift you like wheat" (verse 31). What right did Satan have to make such a demand? Peter had apparently given Satan an open door through pride when he debated with the disciples about which of them was the greatest (Luke 22:24). Even though Peter wholeheartedly intended to stand by his Master to the death (verse 33), Jesus announced that Peter would deny Him three times (verse 34), which he did. It's encouraging to know that Jesus had already prayed for Peter's successful recovery (verse 32).

Ephesians 6:10-17. These verses contain Paul's strong encouragement to believers to "put on the full armor of God, so that you will be able to stand firm against the schemes of the devil" (verse 11). What is the purpose of armor? To prevent the enemy's arrows from penetrating the body and injuring the soldier. If it were impossible for Satan's arrows to penetrate us, there would be no need for us to put on the armor. Paul's teaching about spiritual armor suggests that it is possible for the enemy to penetrate our lives and gain a measure of control.

James 3:14-16. James tells us that if we yield to jealousy and selfish ambition, we may open ourselves to being controlled by wisdom which is "earthly, natural, demonic" (verse 15).

1 Timothy 4:1-3. Paul wrote, "Some will fall away from the faith, paying attention to deceitful spirits and doctrines of demons" (verse 1). Satan can deceive your mind in those areas where you are vulnerable to his control. Evidences of control mentioned here are unbiblical practices in the areas of eating habits and marriage (verse 3).

1 Corinthians 5:1-13. This passage contains Paul's teaching about a Christian man who was living with his father's wife (verse 1). He was a man so deceived by Satan and controlled by immorality that he apparently bragged about his sinful relationship in front of the whole church. Paul's judgment on the matter was severe: "I have decided to deliver such a one to Satan for the destruction of his flesh, so that his spirit may be saved in the day of the Lord Jesus" (verse 5). Paul let Satan have his way with the man for a while in hopes that he would finally say "I've had enough" and repent.

Some people wonder whether a person living this deeply in sin is really a Christian. But if this man had been a non-Christian, Paul would not have corrected him, because the church is only required to discipline its members, not unbelievers. This man was a believer (at least Paul treated him like one) who had allowed himself to become trapped in sexual sin. Paul's hope was that he would experience the natural consequences of his sin, repent, and be set free from his bondage.

Ephesians 4:26,27. Paul instructed, " 'In your anger do not sin': Do not let the sun go down while you are still angry, and do not give the devil a foothold" (NIV). The word *foothold* literally means a "place." Paul is saying that we may give the devil a place in our lives if we fail to speak the truth in love and manage our emotions. Anger which turns to bitterness and unforgiveness is an open door for Satan (2 Corinthians 2:10,11).

1 Peter 5:6-9. Peter warned, "Your adversary, the devil, prowls around like a roaring lion, seeking someone to devour" (verse 8). The word *devour* means to swallow up. To be swallowed up by something certainly conveys the thought of being controlled by it. If believers can't be controlled by Satan, Peter would not need to warn us about the possibility.

Peter's warning suggests two conditions that may open up a believer to Satan's control. In verse 6, we are encouraged to humble ourselves before the Lord. Peter indicates that whenever we resist pride, we resist Satan. And verses 7 and 8 suggest that if we don't learn how to cast our worries on the Lord, we make ourselves easy prey.

Acts 5:1-11. The members of the young Jerusalem church were freely selling their property and giving the profits to the apostles for use in ministry. "But a man named Ananias, with his wife Sapphira, sold a piece of property, and kept back some of the price for himself, with his wife's full knowledge, and bringing a portion of it, he laid it at the apostles' feet. But Peter said, 'Ananias, why has Satan filled your heart to lie to the Holy Spirit and to keep back some of the price of the land?...You have not lied to men but to God'" (verses 1-4).

The problem was not that Ananias and Sapphira kept part of the money, but that they lied about it. They apparently said that what they gave was the total amount they had received. The consequence of the couple's sin was immediate and sobering: They died on the spot (verses 5,10).

This event took place inside the Christian church, and Ananias and Sapphira were obviously members. Why did God so dramatically judge Ananias and Sapphira in the struggling early days of the church? Because He knew what the real battle was going to be for the church. It's still true today—if Satan can get into your church, into your home, or into you undetected and convince you to believe a lie, he can control your life.

Acts 5:11 says, "And great fear came over the whole church." If God were judging someone *outside* the church, why would great fear come over those *inside* the church? There was great fear among *believers* because God had dramatically displayed what He thinks about *believers* who live a lie.

This tough punishment showed that God was emphasizing the importance of truth in the community of believers. Unbelievers lie all the time, but they aren't zapped dead like Ananias and Sapphira were. God was communicating early in the church's history that our major problem is not drugs, sex, or false religions; it's giving in to Satan's deception.

Ananias' problem was that he had allowed Satan's deception to fill (control) his heart. The word *filled* in Acts 5:3 is the same word used in Ephesians 5:18: "Be filled with the Spirit." It is possible for believers to be filled with satanic deception or filled by the Spirit. To whichever source we yield, by that source we shall be filled and controlled. When we allow Satan to deceive us in any area of our life, we are open to his control in that area.

The Devil Did Not Make You Do It!

We can't totally blame Ananias and Sapphira's fall on Satan. We must remember that these two believers willingly participated in the lie which led to their deaths. Peter asked them individually: "Why is it that you have conceived this deed in your heart?"; "Why is it that you have agreed together to put the Spirit of the Lord to the test?" (Acts 5:4,9). Yes, Satan filled their hearts with deception and exercised a measure of control over them in their sin. But he was only able to do so because at some point Ananias and Sapphira opened the door for him.

Don't ever believe someone who says, "The devil made me do it." No, he didn't make us do it; *we* allowed him to do it. Somewhere along the line, we chose to give the devil a foothold. He merely took advantage of the opportunity we gave him. We have all the resources and protection we need to live a victorious life in Christ every day. If we're not living it, it's our choice. When we leave a door open for the devil by not resisting temptation, accusation, or deception, he will enter it. And if we continue to allow him access to that area, he will eventually control it. We won't lose our salvation, but we will lose our daily victory.

Many young Christians today who cannot control their lives in some area sit around blaming themselves instead of solving the problem. They scold themselves and punish themselves for not having the willpower to break a bad habit when instead they should be resisting Satan in an area where he has robbed them of control. Anything bad that you cannot stop doing, or anything good that you cannot make yourself do, is an area of bondage.

If We're Not Responsible, We Will Lose Control

Previously we looked at the believer's protection in the face of demonic attack. We must assume our responsibility because this protection is not something we can take for granted. God's protection depends on our willingness to apply the protection God has provided.

In Romans 13:14 we are told to "put on the Lord Jesus Christ, and make no provision for the flesh in regard to its lusts." But what if we *do* make provision for the flesh by giving Satan an opening in our life through sin? Do we have unlimited protection from Satan's invasion, no matter what we do? No, we must do what God tells us to do so we can take advantage of His protection.

James 4:7 tells us to "resist the devil and he will flee from you." What if we don't resist him? Is he required to run from us if we don't take our stand against him? No, if we don't resist him, he doesn't have to go. God's protection in this area is guaranteed, but we switch on that protection by resisting Satan.

Ephesians 6:10-17 describes the armor of God that we are instructed to put on in order to "stand firm against the schemes of the devil" (verse 11). But if we go into battle without our armor, will God protect us from getting wounded? No, if we fail to cover ourselves with the armor God has provided, we are vulnerable in those exposed areas.

James 4:1 tells us that the source of our quarrels and fights is the evil desires within us. Paul instructs us, "Do not let sin reign in your mortal body so that you obey its evil desires" (Romans 6:12 NIV). The world, the flesh, and the devil are continually at war against the life of the Spirit within us. But what if we don't fight back? Will we still be victorious over the evil desires that try to rule over us? No, they will control us if we fail to halt their invasion by resisting Satan.

Choosing truth, living a righteous life, and putting on the armor of God is each believer's individual responsibility. Mom and Dad, your pastor, and your youth leader are not responsible for you. They can pray for you, encourage you in the faith, and support you. But if you go into the battle without your armor on, you may get hurt. Those who love you may be very concerned for you, but they still can't make those decisions of responsibility for you. Those choices are yours alone.

At this point you may be thinking like the apostle Paul in Romans 7:15, "I am not practicing what I would like to do, but I am doing the very thing I hate." You realize that you have been a target for Satan's temptation, accusation, and deception. You haven't been resisting Satan as you should. You wonder, "Am I stuck in my problems? I have left the door open for Satan, and he has taken advantage of me. Can I get him out of the places he has wormed into?"

The answer is yes! Jesus Christ is the Bondage Breaker. But in order to experience His freedom, we must find the doors we left open through which Satan gained entrance. We must say, "Lord, I confess that I am responsible for giving Satan a foothold in my life, and I renounce the involvement with him which has led to my bondage." We call this process the Steps to Freedom in Christ. Are you ready to be free? Chapter 13 will lead you through the Steps to Freedom, and then you will be free indeed.

Truth Encounter

Read:

Romans 13:14; Ephesians 6:10-17; Romans 6:12

Reflect:

1. In this chapter, we gave some biblical examples of saints who lost control and allowed the enemy to influence them. How was the apostle Peter deceived? (For help, see Luke 22:31-34.)

2. In what way did Satan deceive Ananias and Sapphira? What main issue was God concerned about? (For help, see Acts 5:1-11.)

3. What insights did you gain that will help you stay free from any demonic deceptions or control?

4. What protection has God given us against Satan's deceptions and control?

Respond:

Pray and ask God to reveal to your mind any time in which you might have surrendered to Satan's deception and failed to resist Satan, failed to put on God's armor, or allowed sin to reign in your life. Be sure to confess and renounce any event that comes to mind.

Part 3

Walk Free!

Steps to Freedom in Christ

THIRTEEN

IF YOU HAVE RECEIVED CHRIST as your personal Savior, He has set you free from sin and Satan's power through His victory on the cross and His resurrection. But if you are not *experiencing* freedom in your daily life, it may be because you have not realized who you are in Christ and taken a stand against the devil and his lies. It is your responsibility to do whatever is necessary to maintain a right relationship with God. Your eternal relationship with God is not at stake; you are safe and secure in Christ. But your daily victory in Him will be shaky at best if you fail to claim and maintain your freedom.

In this chapter we want to present seven steps you need to take in order to experience the full freedom and victory that Christ purchased for you on the cross. Don't expect someone else to take these steps for you. This is something you alone must do, even though we strongly recommend that a mature Christian sit with you as you go through these steps (a parent, a trusted friend, a pastor or youth leader, a counselor, or someone else you trust). Your freedom will be the result of what you choose to believe, confess, forgive, renounce, and forsake. No one can believe for you. The battle for your mind can only be won as you personally choose truth.

As you go through these steps, you may experience thoughts like "This isn't going to work" or "God doesn't love me." Those are lies from the enemy. They can only stop you if you believe them. If you are working through these steps alone, don't pay attention to Satan's lies. If another Christian is working with you as we recommend, share with that person any thoughts that tempt you to give up. As soon as you uncover the lie, the power of Satan is broken.

Remember that Satan will be defeated only if you confront him aloud. He doesn't have to obey your thoughts. Only God perfectly knows what is going on in your mind. As you take each step, it is important that you submit to God in your heart and then resist the devil by reading aloud each prayer and statement (James 4:7).

Here is a prayer to get you started. Pray it out loud from your heart:

> *Dear heavenly Father, I know that You are here in this room and present in my life. You are the only all-knowing, all-powerful, ever-present God. I desperately need You because without Jesus I can do nothing.*
>
> *I believe the Bible because it tells me what is really true. I refuse to believe the lies of Satan. I stand in the truth that all authority in heaven and on earth has been given to the risen Christ. I ask You to protect my thoughts and mind, to fill me with Your Holy Spirit, and to lead me into all truth. I pray for Your complete protection. In Jesus' name I pray, amen.*

If a Christian friend or counselor is with you, he or she may declare the following for you; or else declare it for yourself aloud:

In the name and the authority of the Lord Jesus Christ, we command Satan and all evil spirits to let go of (name) in order that (name) can be free to know and choose to do the will of God. As children of God seated with Christ in the heavenlies, we agree that every enemy of the Lord Jesus Christ be bound to silence in (name). We say to Satan and all of his evil workers that you cannot inflict any pain or in any way stop or hinder God's will from being done today in (name).

Step 1: Counterfeit vs. Real

The first step to freedom in Christ is to renounce (turn your back on) any present or past involvement with satanically inspired occult practices or false religions. You must renounce any activity and group that denies Jesus Christ, tries to direct your life through any source other than the Bible, or requires secret initiations, ceremonies, promises, or pacts (covenants). No Christian has any business being part of a group that is not completely open about what it does (1 John 1:5,7).

You must not only choose truth, but reject Satan and his lies. There is no middle ground. Jesus said, "He who is not with Me is against Me" (Luke 11:23). There are not *many* paths to God; there is only *one* way (John 14:6). Other religions and cults may talk about Jesus, but they present Him in another way than He is presented in the Bible. They may agree that Jesus lived in history, but fail to call Him the Son of God.

In order to help you evaluate your spiritual experiences, fill out the following "Non-Christian Spiritual Checklist." The list will help you identify any non-Christian practices you have been involved in. If the list does not include something you have done that you feel was a non-Christian practice, be sure to add it. Even if you were "innocently" involved in something, or only watched someone else who was involved, you should write it on your list and renounce it just in case you gave Satan a foothold without realizing it.

Don't be surprised if you feel some resistance as you complete this step. Satan doesn't want you to be free, and he will do whatever he can do to keep you from claiming your freedom.

As you go through this step, pray in the following way:

> *Dear heavenly Father, reveal to me anything that I have done or that someone has done to me that is spiritually wrong. Show me how I have been involved with any cults, false religions, occult/satanic practices, or false teachers, whether I knew it or not. I want to experience Your freedom and do Your will. I ask this in Jesus' name, amen.*

Non-Christian Spiritual Checklist

Circle any of the following activities in which you have been involved in any way.

OCCULT

out-of-body experience

Ouija board

Bloody Mary

Magic Eight Ball

table lifting or body lifting

using spells or curses

automatic writing

spirit guides

fortune-telling

objects of worship, crystals, or good luck charms

others:

palm-reading

Astrology or horoscopes or both

hypnosis

seances

Islam

black or white magic

Dungeons & Dragons

other fantasy games

tarot cards

blood pacts or cutting yourself in a destructive way

CULT	OTHER RELIGIONS
Mormonism	Zen Buddhism
Jehovah's Witnesses	Hinduism
New Age	Islam
New Age medicine	martial arts
Masons	transcendental meditation
Scientology	yoga
Christian Science	others:
others:	

Write down the titles of any anti-Christian movies, music, books, magazines, comic books, TV programs, video games, and so on that may have influenced you in a wrong way.

movies:

music:

books, magazines, comic books:

TV programs, video games:

1. Have you ever felt, heard, or seen a spiritual being in your room?

2. Have you had an imaginary friend who talks to you?

3. Have you ever heard voices in your head or had repeating, nagging thoughts like, "I'm dumb," "I'm ugly," "I can't do anything right," and so on as if there were a conversation going on in your head?

4. Have you or has anyone in your family ever consulted a medium, spiritist, or channeler?

5. What other spiritual experiences have you had that could be considered out of the ordinary (telepathy,

speaking in a trance, knowing something supernaturally, and so on)?

6. Have you ever been involved in satanic worship of any form or attended a concert where Satan was the focus?

When you are sure that your list is complete, confess and renounce each involvement by praying aloud the following prayer, repeating it separately for each item on your list:

> *Lord, I confess that I have participated in _____. Thank You for Your forgiveness and I renounce _____ as a counterfeit to true Christianity.*

After you have gone through each item that God has brought to your mind, finish with this prayer:

> *Lord, I confess each of these offenses to You as sin. I know that they were wrong. Thank You for Your forgiveness. I renounce all my involvement with these offenses, and I cancel out any and all ground that the enemy gained in my life through these activities. In Jesus' name, amen.*

Renouncing Wrong Priorities

Who or what is most important to us becomes that which we worship. Our thoughts, love, devotion, trust, adoration, and obedience are directed to this object above all others. This object of worship is truly our God or god(s).

We were created to worship the true and living God. In fact, the Father seeks those who will worship Him in spirit and in truth (John 4:23). As children of God, "we know also that the Son of God has come and has given us understanding, so that we may know him who is true. And we are in him who is true—even in his Son Jesus Christ. He is the true God and eternal life" (1 John 5:20 NIV).

The apostle John follows the above passage with a warning: "Little children, guard yourselves from idols" (1 John 5:21). An idol is a false god, any object of worship other than the true and living God. Though we may not bow down to statues, it is easy for people and things of this world to subtly become more important to us than the Lord. The following prayer expresses the commitment of a heart that chooses to "worship the Lord your God, and serve Him only" (Matthew 4:10).

> *Dear Lord God, I know how easy it is to allow other things and other people to become more important to me than You. I also know that this is terribly offensive in Your holy eyes. You have commanded that I "shall have no other gods" before You.*
>
> *I confess to You that I have not loved You with all my heart and soul and mind. As a result, I have sinned against You, violating the first and greatest commandment. I repent of and turn away from this idolatry and now choose to return to You, Lord Jesus, as my first love.*
>
> *Please reveal to my mind now any and all idols in my life. I want to renounce each of them and, in so doing, cancel out any and all ground Satan may have gained in my life through my idolatry. In the name of Jesus, the true God, amen.*
>
> (See Exodus 20:3; Matthew 22:37;
> Revelation 2:4,5)

The checklist below may help you recognize those areas where things or people have become more important to you than the true God, Jesus Christ. Notice that most (if not all) of the areas listed below are not evil in themselves; they become idols when they usurp God's rightful place as Lord of our lives.

- Ambition
- Food or any substance
- Money/possessions
- Computers/games/software
- Financial security
- Rock stars/media celebrities/athletes
- Church activities
- TV/movies/music/other media
- Sports or physical fitness
- Fun/pleasure
- Ministry
- Appearance/image
- Work
- Busyness/activity
- Friends
- Power/control
- Boyfriend/girlfriend
- Popularity/opinion of others
- Spouse
- Knowledge/being right
- Hobbies
- Parents

Use the following prayer to renounce any areas of idolatry or wrong priority the Holy Spirit brings to your mind.

In the name of the true and living God, Jesus Christ,
I renounce my worship of the false god of (name the
idol). I choose to worship only You, Lord. I ask You,
Father, to enable me to keep this area of (name the
idol) in its proper place in my life.

Satanic Ritual Involvement

Have you been involved in satanic rituals or heavy occult activity? Or have you experienced severe nightmares, suggesting that satanic, occult activity in your past has been blocked from your memory? All satanic rituals, covenants (promises), and assignments must be specifically renounced as the Lord allows you to remember them.

Step 2: Deception vs. Truth

The truth is found in God's Word, the Bible. God desires us to plant His truth in our hearts so we live the truth (Psalm 51:6). When David lived a lie, he really suffered. When he finally found freedom by agreeing with the truth, he wrote, "How blessed is the man…in whose spirit there is no deceit" (Psalm 32:2). We must get rid of anything false in our lives and speak the truth in love (Ephesians 4:15,25).

Begin this important step by reading aloud the following prayer:

Dear heavenly Father, I know that You want me to
face the truth and that I must be honest with You. I
know that choosing to believe the truth will set me
free. I have been deceived by Satan, the father of lies,
and I have deceived myself. I thought I could hide it
from You, but You see everything and still love me.

I pray in the name of the Lord Jesus Christ, asking You to rebuke all of Satan's demons through Your righteous Son Jesus, who shed His blood on the cross and rose from the dead for me. I have asked Jesus into my life, and I am Your child. Therefore, by the authority of the Lord Jesus Christ, I command all evil spirits to leave me.

I ask the Holy Spirit to lead me into all truth. I ask You to look deep inside me and know my heart. Show me if there is anything in me that I am trying to hide, because I want to be free. In Jesus' name I pray, amen.

(See John 8:32; 8:44; 1 John 1:8;
Psalm 139:23,24)

There are many ways in which Satan, "the god of this world" (2 Corinthians 4:4) seeks to deceive us. Just as he did with Eve, the devil attempts to convince us to rely on ourselves and to try to get our needs met through the world around us, rather than trusting in our Father in heaven.

Ways You Can Be Deceived by the World

- Believing that acquiring money and things will bring lasting happiness (Matthew 13:22; 1 Timothy 6:10)
- Believing that consuming food and alcohol excessively will make me happy (Proverbs 20:1; 23:19-21)
- Believing that a great body and personality will get me what I want (Proverbs 31:30; 1 Peter 3:3,4)
- Believing that gratifying sexual lust will bring lasting satisfaction (Ephesians 4:22; 1 Peter 2:11)
- Believing that I can sin and get away with it, and not have it affect my heart (Hebrews 3:12,13)

- Believing that I need more than what God has given me in Christ (2 Corinthians 11:2-4,13-15)
- Believing that I can do whatever I want and no one can touch me (Proverbs 16:18; Obadiah 3; 1 Peter 5:5)
- Believing that unrighteous people who refuse to accept Christ go to heaven anyway (1 Corinthians 6:9-11)
- Believing that I can hang around bad company and not become corrupted (1 Corinthians 15:33,34)
- Believing that there are no consequences on earth for my sin (Galatians 6:7,8)
- Believing that I must gain the approval of certain people in order to be happy (Galatians 1:10)
- Believing that I must measure up to certain standards in order to feel good about myself (Galatians 3:2,3; 5:1)

Lord, I confess that I have been deceived by _____. I thank You for Your forgiveness, and I commit myself to believing only Your truth. In Jesus' name, amen.

Take some time at this point to think of other evil tricks Satan has used to deceive you. Have you been listening to false teachers or deceiving spirits? Have you been living under self-deception? Have you used excuses to defend your behavior? Now that you are alive in Christ and forgiven, you don't have to live a lie, and you don't have to defend yourself! Check those below that apply to you.

Ways You Can Deceive Yourself
- Hear God's Word but not do it (James 1:22; 4:17)
- Say you have no sin (1 John 1:8)

- Think you are something you are really not (Galatians 6:3)
- Think you are wise in the things of the world (1 Corinthians 3:18,19)
- Think you will not reap what you sow (Galatians 6:7)
- Think that unholy people will share in God's kingdom (1 Corinthians 6:9)
- Think you can be with bad company and it won't have any influence on you (1 Corinthians 15:33)

Wrong Ways to Defend Yourself

- Refuse to face the real things that have happened to you
- Escape from the real world
- Withdraw to avoid rejection
- Revert to a less threatening time
- Take out frustrations on others
- Blame others
- Look for an excuse
- Lying

For those things that have been true in your life, pray aloud:

> *Lord, I agree that I have been deceived in the area of _____. Thank You for forgiving me. I commit myself to know and follow Your truth.*

Choosing the truth may be hard for you if you have been believing lies for many years. You may need some ongoing counseling to help weed out any defense mechanisms you have relied on to cope with life. Every Christian needs to learn that Christ is the only defense he or she needs. Realizing that you are already forgiven and accepted by God through Christ will help free you up to place all your dependence on Him.

Ways That We Can Be Deceived About God

Faith is the biblical response to the truth, and believing what God says is a choice we all can make. If you say, "I wish I could believe God, but I just can't," you are being deceived. Of course you can believe God, because what God says is always true.

Sometimes we are greatly hindered from walking by faith in our Father God because of lies we have believed about Him. We are to have a healthy fear of God (awe of His holiness, power, and presence), but we are not to be afraid of Him.

Romans 8:15 says, "You have not received a spirit of slavery leading to fear again, but you have received a spirit of adoption as sons by which we cry out, 'Abba! Father!'" The following exercise will help break the chains of those lies and enable you to begin to experience that intimate "Abba, Father" relationship with Him.

Work your way down the lists on page 206, one by one, left to right. Begin each one with the statement in bold at the top of that list. Read through the lists *out loud*.

Ways That Our Fears Deceive Us

A central part of walking in the truth and rejecting deception is to deal with the fears that plague our lives. First Peter 5:8 says that our enemy, the devil, prowls around like a roaring lion, seeking people to devour. Just as a lion's roar strikes terror in the hearts of those who hear it, so Satan uses fear to try to paralyze Christians. Satan's intimidation tactics

I renounce the lie that my Father God is...	**I joyfully accept the truth that my Father God is...**
1. distant and uninterested	1. intimate and involved (Psalm 139:1-18)
2. insensitive and uncaring	2. kind and compassionate (Psalm 103:8-14)
3. stern and demanding	3. accepting and filled with joy and love (Zephaniah 3:17; Romans 15:7)
4. passive and cold	4. warm and affectionate (Isaiah 40:11; Hosea 11:3,4)
5. absent or too busy for me	5. always with me and eager to be with me (Jeremiah 31:20; Ezekiel 34:11-16; Hebrews 13:5)
6. never satisfied with what I do, impatient, or angry	6. patient and slow to anger (Exodus 34:6; 2 Peter 3:9)
7. mean, cruel, or abusive	7. loving, gentle, and protective of me (Psalm 18:2; Jeremiah 31:3; Isaiah 42:3)
8. trying to take all the fun out of life	8. trustworthy and wants to give me a full life; His will is good, perfect, and acceptable (Lamentations 3:22,23; John 10:10; Romans 12:1,2)
9. controlling or manipulative	9. full of grace and mercy; He gives me freedom to fail (Luke 15:11-16; Hebrews 4:15,16)
10. condemning or unforgiving	10. tenderhearted and forgiving; His heart and arms are always open to me (Psalm 130:1-4; Luke 15:17-24)
11. nit-picking, exacting, or perfectionistic	11. committed to my growth and proud of me as His growing child (Romans 8:28,29; 2 Corinthians 7:4; Hebrews 12:5-11)

I am the apple of His eye!
(Deuteronomy 32:10 NIV)

are designed to rob us of faith in God and to drive us to try to get our needs met through the world or the flesh. Fear weakens us, causes us to be self-centered, and clouds our minds so that all we can think about is the thing that frightens us. But fear can only control us if we let it.

God, however, does not want us to be mastered by anything, including fear (1 Corinthians 6:12). Jesus Christ is to be our only Master (John 13:13; 2 Timothy 2:21). In order to begin to experience freedom from the bondage of fear and experience the ability to walk by faith in God, pray the following prayer from your heart:

> *Dear heavenly Father, I confess to You that I have listened to the devil's roar and have allowed fear to master me. I have not always walked by faith in You but instead have focused on my feelings and circumstances. Thank You for forgiving me for my unbelief.*
>
> *Right now I renounce the spirit of fear and affirm the truth that You have not given me a spirit of fear but of power, love, and a sound mind. Lord, please reveal to my mind now all the fears that have been controlling me so I can renounce them and be free to walk by faith in You.*
>
> *I thank You for the freedom You give me to walk by faith and not by fear. In Jesus' powerful name I pray, amen.*
>
> (See 2 Corinthians 4:16-18; 5:7;
> 2 Timothy 1:7)

The following list may help you recognize some of the fears the devil has used to keep you from walking by faith. Check the ones that apply to your life. Write down any others that the Spirit of God brings to your mind. Then, one by one, renounce those fears out loud, using the suggested renunciation after the list.

- Fear of death
- Fear of Satan
- Fear of failure
- Fear of rejection by people
- Fear of disapproval
- Fear of becoming/being homosexual
- Fear of financial problems
- Fear of never getting married
- Fear of the death of a loved one
- Fear of being a hopeless case
- Fear of losing salvation
- Fear of having committed the unpardonable sin
- Fear of not being loved by God
- Fear of never loving or being loved by others
- Fear of embarrassment
- Fear of being victimized by crime
- Fear of marriage
- Fear of divorce
- Fear of going crazy
- Fear of pain/illness
- Fear of the future
- Fear of confrontation
- Fear of specific individuals (list their names)
- Other specific fears that come to mind now:

*I renounce the (name the fear) because God has not
given me a spirit of fear. I choose to live by faith in
the God who has promised to protect me and meet
all my needs as I walk by faith in Him.*

(See Psalm 27:1; Matthew 6:33,34;
2 Timothy 1:7)

After you have finished renouncing all the specific fears
you have allowed to control you, pray the following prayer:

*Dear heavenly Father, I thank You that You are
trustworthy. I choose to believe You, even when my
feelings and circumstances tell me to fear. You have
told me not to fear, for You are with me; to not anx-
iously look about me, for You are my God. You will
strengthen me, help me, and surely uphold me with
Your righteous right hand. I pray this with faith in
the name of Jesus my Master, amen.*

(See Isaiah 41:10)

Faith Must Be Based on the Truth of God's Word

The New Age movement has twisted the concept of faith
by saying that we make something true by believing it. No,
we can't create reality with our minds; only God can do that.
We can only *face* reality with our minds. Faith is choosing to
believe and act upon what God says, regardless of feelings or
circumstances. Believing something, however, does not
make it true. *It's true; therefore, we choose to believe it.*

Just "having faith" is not enough. The key question is
whether the object of your faith is trustworthy. If the object
of your faith is not reliable, then no amount of believing will
change it. That is why our faith must be in the solid rock of

God and His Word. That is the only way to live a responsible and fruitful life. On the other hand, if what you believe in is not true, then how you end up living will not be right.

For generations, Christians have known the importance of publicly declaring what they believe. Read aloud the following "Statement of Truth," thinking about what you are saying. You may find it very helpful to read it daily for several weeks to renew your mind with the truth and replace any lies you may be believing.

Statement of Truth

1. I believe that there is only one true and living God (Exodus 20:2,3), who exists as the Father, Son, and Holy Spirit. He alone is worthy of all honor, praise, and glory. I believe that He made all things and holds all things together (Colossians 1:16,17).

2. I recognize Jesus Christ as the Messiah, the Word who became flesh and lived with us (John 1:1,14). I believe that He came to destroy the works of Satan (1 John 3:8).

3. I believe that God showed how much He loves me by sending Christ to die for me, even though I was sinful (Romans 5:8). I believe that God rescued me from the kingdom of darkness and brought me into the kingdom of His Son, who has forgiven my sins and set me free (Colossians 1:13,14).

4. I believe I am spiritually strong because Jesus is my strength. I have the authority to stand against Satan because I am a child of God (1 John 3:1-3). I believe that I was saved by the grace of God through faith, that it was a gift and not the result of any works on my part (Ephesians 2:8).

5. I choose to be strong in the Lord and in the strength of His might (Ephesians 6:10). I put no confidence in the flesh (Philippians 3:3), for the weapons of our warfare are not of the flesh (2 Corinthians 10:4). I put on the whole armor of God (Ephesians 6:10-17), and I resolve to stand firm in my faith and resist the evil one.

6. I believe that apart from Christ I can do nothing (John 15:5), so I will depend totally on Him. I choose to remain in Christ in order to bear much fruit and glorify the Lord (John 15:8). I announce to Satan that Jesus is my Lord (1 Corinthians 12:3), and I reject any counterfeit gifts or works of Satan in my life.

7. I believe that the truth will set me free (John 8:32). I stand against Satan's lies by taking every thought captive in obedience to Christ (2 Corinthians 10:5). I believe that the Bible is the only reliable guide for my life (2 Timothy 3:15,16). I choose to speak the truth in love (Ephesians 4:15).

8. I choose to give my body to God to be used for righteousness, a living and holy sacrifice, and I choose to renew my mind by God's Word (Romans 6:13; 12:1,2). I have put off the old self with its evil practices and have put on the new self (Colossians 3:9,10). I am a new creature in Christ (2 Corinthians 5:17).

9. I ask my heavenly Father to fill me with His Holy Spirit (Ephesians 5:18), to lead me into all truth (John 16:13), and to give me power to live above sin and not carry out the desires of the flesh (Galatians 5:16). I crucify the flesh and choose to be led by and obey the Holy Spirit (Galatians 5:24,25).

10. I renounce all selfish goals and choose the ultimate goal of love (1 Timothy 1:5). I choose to obey the two greatest commandments: to love the Lord my God with

all my heart, soul, and mind, and to love others in the same way I love myself (Matthew 22:37-39).

11. I believe that Jesus has all authority in heaven and on earth (Matthew 28:18) and that He rules over everything (Colossians 2:10). I believe that Satan and his demons are subject to me in Christ because I am a member of His body (Ephesians 1:19-23). I will obey God's command to submit to Him and to resist the devil (James 4:7). I command Satan in the name of Christ to leave my presence.

Step 3: Bitterness vs. Forgiveness

If you do not forgive people who hurt you or offend you, you are a wide-open target for Satan's attacks. You need to forgive others so that Satan can't take advantage of you (2 Corinthians 2:10,11). We are to forgive others because God has shown us mercy and has forgiven us (Luke 6:36; Ephesians 4:31,32).

Ask God to bring to your mind those people you need to forgive, as you read the following prayer out loud:

> *Dear heavenly Father, thank You for Your kindness and patience that led me to turn from my sin. I have not always been kind, patient, and loving toward others, especially those who have hurt me. I have been bitter and resentful. I give You my emotions, and ask You to bring to the surface all my painful memories so I can choose to forgive from my heart. I ask You to bring to my mind the people I need to forgive. I ask this in the precious name of Jesus, who will heal me from my hurts, amen.*
>
> (See Romans 2:4; Matthew 18:35)

On a sheet of paper, make a list of the names that come to mind. Don't be surprised if your parents are near the top.

With 95 percent of the people we lead through these steps, the first two names on the list are their parents.

The two most overlooked names on the list are self and God. Forgiving yourself for your failures shows that you accept God's cleansing and forgiveness. Is it right to forgive God? He certainly hasn't done anything wrong—He can't. But maybe you cried out to Him with a need, and He didn't seem to answer, so you are angry with Him. You may need to release Him for not living up to your false expectations.

Before you pray to forgive the people on your list, here are a few important things you need to understand about forgiveness:

Forgiveness is not forgetting. People who try to forget the pain caused by others often find they cannot. God says that He will remember our sins no more (Hebrews 10:17). But God knows everything, and He can't forget. "Remember our sins no more" means that God will never use our sins against us (Psalm 103:12). You may not be able to forget your past, but you can be free from it. When we bring up the past and use it against others, we haven't forgiven them.

Forgiveness is a choice. We may feel it's impossible to forgive someone. But since God requires us to forgive, it is something we *can* do. God would never require us to do something we cannot do. We forgive by *choosing* to forgive.

Forgiveness means giving up on revenge. Forgiveness is sometimes hard for us because we want revenge for the hurts we have suffered. But we are told never to take our own revenge (Romans 12:19). "Why should I let them off the hook?" we argue. When we forgive, we let them off *our* hook, but they aren't off *God's* hook. He will deal with them fairly, something we can't do.

If we don't let the offenders off our hook, we are hooked to them and to our hurts. We can stop the pain by letting go of the problem. We don't forgive someone just for their sake; we do it for *our* sake so we can be free. Your need to forgive isn't an issue between you and the person who hurt you; it's between you and God.

Forgiveness is agreeing to live with the consequences of another person's sin. It costs us something to forgive. We pay the price for the hurt we forgive. We are going to live with the consequences whether we want to or not. Our only choice is whether we will do so in the bondage of bitterness or the freedom of forgiveness.

How do we forgive from our heart? First, we must admit the hurt and hatred we feel, instead of burying them deep inside. If forgiveness doesn't include our emotions, it will be incomplete. You may not know how to deal with your feelings, but God does. Let Him bring the pain to the surface so He can deal with it. This is where the healing begins.

Since God has forgiven everyone on your list, you can too. This doesn't mean that you have to put up with continuing sin. It's possible to forgive the sins of the past and take a stand against the sins of the present.

Don't wait to forgive until you *feel* like forgiving. You will never get there. Feelings take time to heal; this will happen after the choice to forgive is made and Satan has lost his place (Ephesians 4:26,27).

For each person on your list pray aloud:

> Lord, I forgive (<u>name</u>) for (<u>specifically name all his</u> <u>or her offenses and your painful memories that</u> <u>come to your mind</u>).

Keep praying about each person until you are sure that all the pain you remember has been dealt with. Positive feelings will follow in time; freeing yourself from the hurts of the past is the important issue.

Step 4: Rebellion vs. Submission

We live in rebellious times. Many young people today don't respect or submit to the authorities God has placed over them. Christians are no exception. But rebelling against God, parents, and other authorities gives Satan an opportunity to attack.

The Bible tells us we have two responsibilities to the human authorities God has placed over us: to pray for them and to submit to them. The only time God permits us to disobey earthly leaders is when they order us to do something morally wrong before God. There are times when parents, other relatives, teachers, and others abuse their authority and break the laws that are ordained by God to protect innocent people. In such cases, we need to seek help for our protection. When people in authority abuse their positions and ask us to break God's law or compromise our commitment to Him, we need to obey God, not people.

Study the following verses to understand how God wants us to respond to authority: civil government (Romans 13:1-7; 1 Timothy 2:1-4; 1 Peter 2:13-17); parents (Ephesians 6:1-3); employer (1 Peter 2:18-21); church leaders (Hebrews 13:17). Now pray the following prayer aloud:

> *Dear heavenly Father, You have said in the Bible that rebellion is as bad as witchcraft and disobedience is as sinful as serving false gods. I know that I have disobeyed You by rebelling in my heart against You and against those people You have put in authority over me. I ask Your forgiveness for my rebellion.*

*By the shed blood of the Lord Jesus Christ, I resist
all evil spirits that took advantage of my rebellion. I
pray that You will show me all the ways I have been
rebellious. I choose to adopt a submissive spirit and
servant's heart. In the name of Jesus Christ my Lord,
amen.*

(See 1 Samuel 15:23)

As you prayerfully look over the next list, allow the Lord
to show you any *specific* ways in which you have been rebellious to authority.

- Civil government (including traffic laws, tax laws, attitude toward government officials) (Romans 13:1-7; 1 Timothy 2:1-4; 1 Peter 2:13-17)
- Parents, stepparents, or legal guardians (Ephesians 6:1-3)
- Teachers, coaches, school officials (Romans 13:1-4)
- Employers (past and present) (1 Peter 2:18-23)
- Church leaders (Hebrews 13:17)
- God (Daniel 9:5,9)

For each way in which the Spirit of God brings to your
mind that you have been rebellious, use the following prayer
to specifically confess that sin:

*Lord, I confess that I have been rebellious toward
(name) by (say what you did specifically). Thank
You for forgiving my rebellion. I choose now to be
submissive and obedient to Your Word. In Jesus'
name I pray, amen.*

Step 5: Pride vs. Humility

Pride is a killer. Pride says, "I can do it! I can get myself out of this mess without God or anyone else's help." Oh no, we can't! We absolutely need God, and we desperately need each other. Paul wrote: "We...worship in the Spirit of God and glory in Christ Jesus and put no confidence in the flesh" (Philippians 3:3). Humility is confidence properly placed. We are to "be strong in the Lord and in the strength of His might" (Ephesians 6:10). James 4:6-10 and 1 Peter 5:1-10 tell us that spiritual problems will follow when we are proud.

Use the following prayer to express your commitment to live humbly before God:

> *Dear heavenly Father, You have said that pride goes before destruction and an arrogant spirit before stumbling. I confess that I have been thinking mainly of myself and not of others. I have not denied myself, picked up my cross daily, and followed You. I have believed that I am the only one who cares about me, so I must take care of myself. I have turned away from You and have not let You love me.*
>
> *I am tired of living for myself and by myself. I now confess that I have sinned against You by placing my will before Yours and by centering my life around myself instead of You. I renounce my pride and selfishness. I cancel any ground gained by the enemies of the Lord Jesus Christ. I ask You to fill me with Your Holy Spirit so I can do Your will. I give my heart to You and stand against all the ways that Satan attacks me.*
>
> *I ask You to show me how to live for others. I now choose to make other people more important than myself and to make You the most important of all.*

*I ask this in the name of Christ Jesus my Lord,
amen.*

(See Proverbs 16:18; Matthew 16:24;
Romans 12:10)

Having made that commitment, allow God to show you any specific areas in your life where you have been prideful. Check those areas that apply to you.

- I have a stronger desire to do my will than God's will.
- I rely on my own strength rather than God's.
- Too often I think my ideas are better than other people's.
- I want to control others rather than develop self-control.
- Sometimes I consider myself more important than others.
- Sometimes I find it difficult to admit I was wrong.
- I am often a people-pleaser instead of a God-pleaser.
- I am overconcerned about getting the credit I deserve.
- I often think I am more humble than other people.
- I often believe I am smarter than my parents.
- I often feel my needs are more important than the needs of others.
- Other:

For each statement that is true of you, pray the following prayer aloud:

> *Lord, I agree I have been prideful in the area of
> _____. Please forgive me for my pride. I choose to
> humble myself and place all my confidence in You.
> In Jesus' name, amen.*

Dealing with Prejudice and Bigotry

Pride is the original sin of Lucifer. It sets one person or group against another. Satan's strategy is always to divide and conquer, but God has given us a ministry of reconciliation (2 Corinthians 5:19). Take a look for a moment at the work of Christ in breaking down the long-standing barrier of racial prejudice between Jews and Gentiles:

> For [Christ] is our peace, who has made the two one and has destroyed the barrier, the dividing wall of hostility, by abolishing in his flesh the law with its commandments and regulations. His purpose was to create in himself one new man out of the two, thus making peace, and in this one body to reconcile both of them to God through the cross, by which he put to death their hostility. He came and preached peace to you who were far away and peace to those who were near. For through him we both have access to the Father by one Spirit (Ephesians 2:14-18 NIV).

Many times we deny that there is prejudice or bigotry in our hearts, yet "nothing in all creation is hidden from God's sight. Everything is uncovered and laid bare before the eyes of him to whom we must give account" (Hebrews 4:13 NIV). The following is a prayer that asks God to shine His light upon your heart and reveal any area of proud prejudice:

> *Dear heavenly Father, I know that You love all people equally and that You do not play favorites. You accept people from every nation who fear You and do what is right. You do not judge them based on skin color, race, how much money they have, ethnic background, gender, what church they go to, or any other worldly matter.*

> *I confess that I have too often prejudged others or thought of myself as superior because of these things. I have not always been a minister of reconciliation, but have promoted division through my attitudes, words, and deeds. I repent of all hateful bigotry and proud prejudice, and I ask You, Lord, to now show to my mind all the ways this kind of pride has polluted my heart and mind. In Jesus' name, amen.*
>
> (See Acts 10:34; 2 Corinthians 5:16)

For each area of prejudice, superiority, or bigotry that the Lord brings to mind, pray the following prayer out loud from your heart:

> *I confess and renounce the prideful sin of prejudice against (name the group). I thank You for Your forgiveness, Lord, and ask now that You would change my heart and make me a loving agent of reconciliation with (name the group). In Jesus' name, amen.*

Step 6: Bondage vs. Freedom

The next step to freedom deals with sins that have become habits. Teens who have been caught in the trap of sin-confess-sin-confess may need to follow the suggestion of James 5:16: "Confess your sins to one another, and pray for one another so that you may be healed. The effective prayer of a righteous man can accomplish much." Find a spiritually mature person who will hold you up in prayer and check up on you from time to time. Others may only need the assurance of 1 John 1:9: "If we confess our sins, He is faithful and righteous to forgive us our sins and to cleanse us from all unrighteousness."

Whether you need to confess to others or just to God, pray the following prayer:

> Dear heavenly Father, You have said, "Put on the Lord Jesus Christ, and make no provision for the flesh in regard to its lusts" [Romans 13:14]. I understand that I have given in to fleshly lusts, which wage war against my soul. I thank You that in Christ my sins are forgiven; but I have broken Your holy law and given the enemy an opportunity to wage war in my body.
>
> I come before Your presence to admit these sins and to seek Your cleansing that I may be freed from the bondage of sin. I now ask You to reveal to my mind the ways that I have broken Your moral law and disappointed the Holy Spirit. In Jesus' precious name I pray, amen.
>
> (See 1 Peter 2:11; Romans 6:12,13;
> James 4:1; 1 Peter 5:8; 1 John 1:9)

There are many sins of the flesh that can control us. The following list contains many of them, but a prayerful examination of Mark 7:20-23, Galatians 5:19-21, Ephesians 4:25-31, and other Scripture passages will help you to be even more thorough.

Look over the list on page 222 and the Scriptures just listed and ask the Holy Spirit to bring to your mind the sins you need to confess. He may reveal others to you as well. For each one the Lord shows you, pray a prayer of confession from your heart. There is a sample prayer following the list. (*Note:* Sexual sins, eating disorders, substance abuse, abortion, suicidal tendencies, and perfectionism will be dealt with later in this step.

Further counseling help may be necessary to find complete healing and freedom in these and other areas.)

- Stealing
- Jealousy/envy
- Complaining/criticism
- Lustful actions
- Gossip/slander
- Swearing
- Apathy/laziness
- Lying
- Hatred
- Anger
- Lustful thoughts
- Drunkenness
- Cheating
- Procrastination
- Greed/materialism
- Others:

> *Lord, I confess that I have committed the sin of (<u>name the sin</u>). Thank You for Your forgiveness and cleansing. I now turn away from this sin and turn to You, Lord. Strengthen me by Your Holy Spirit to obey You. In Jesus' name, amen.*

Wrong Sexual Uses of Our Body

It is our responsibility not to allow sin to control us by using our body as an instrument of unrighteousness (Romans

6:12,13). If you are struggling with habitual sexual sins (pornography, masturbation, sexual promiscuity, petting), pray as follows:

> *Lord, I ask You to reveal to my mind every sexual use of my body as an instrument of unrighteousness. In Jesus' precious name I pray, amen.*

As the Lord brings to your mind every wrong sexual use of your body, whether it was done to you (for example, rape, incest, or any sexual molestation) or done willingly by you, renounce *every occasion.*

> *Lord, I renounce (<u>name the specific use of your body</u>) with (<u>name the person</u>), and I renounce any bonding that may have taken place.*

Now commit your body to the Lord by praying:

> *Lord, I renounce all these uses of my body as an instrument of unrighteousness, and I confess any willful participation. I now present my body to You as a living sacrifice, holy and acceptable to You, and I reserve the sexual use of my body for only the way You intended. I renounce the lie of Satan that my body is not clean, that it is dirty or in any way unacceptable as a result of my past sexual experiences.*
>
> *Lord, I thank You that You have totally cleansed and forgiven me, that You love and accept me unconditionally. Therefore, I can accept myself. And I choose to do so, to accept myself and my body as cleansed. In Jesus' name, amen.*

Special Prayers for Special Needs

Homosexuality

> Lord, I renounce the lie that You have created me
> or anyone else to be homosexual, and I agree that
> You clearly forbid homosexual behavior. I accept
> myself as a child of God and declare that You cre-
> ated me a man (or woman). I renounce any
> bondages of Satan that have perverted my relation-
> ships with others. I announce that I am free to relate
> to the opposite sex in the way You intended. In Jesus'
> name, amen.

Abortion

> Lord, I confess that I was not a proper guardian and
> keeper of the life You entrusted to me, and I ask Your
> forgiveness. I choose to accept Your forgiveness by
> forgiving myself, and I now commit that child to
> You for Your care in eternity. In Jesus' name, amen.

Suicidal Tendencies

> I renounce the lie that I can find peace and freedom
> by taking my own life. Satan is a thief, and he comes
> to steal, kill, and destroy. I choose life in Christ, who
> said He came to give me life and to give it abun-
> dantly.

Eating Disorders or Self-Mutilation

> I renounce the lie that my value as a person is
> dependent on how I look on the outside. I renounce
> cutting or abusing myself, vomiting, starving myself,
> or using laxatives as a means of cleansing myself of
> evil, and I announce that only the blood of the Lord
> Jesus Christ can cleanse me from my sin.

> *I accept the reality that there may be sin present in me because of the lies I have believed and the wrongful use of my body, but I renounce the lie that I am evil or that any part of my body is evil. I announce the truth that I am totally accepted by Christ, just as I am.*

Substance Abuse

> *Lord, I confess that I have misused substances [alcohol, tobacco, food, prescription or street drugs] for the purpose of pleasure, to escape reality, or to cope with difficult problems. I confess that I have abused my body and programmed my mind in a harmful way. I have not allowed Your Holy Spirit to guide me.*
>
> *I ask Your forgiveness, and I renounce any satanic connection or influence in my life through my misuse of drugs. I cast my cares onto Christ who loves me, and I commit myself to no longer give in to substance abuse but to follow the Holy Spirit's leading. I ask You, heavenly Father, to fill me with Your Holy Spirit. In Jesus' name, amen.*

After you have confessed all known sin, pray:

> *I now confess these sins to You and claim, through the blood of the Lord Jesus Christ, my forgiveness and cleansing. I cancel all ground that evil spirits have gained through my willful involvement in sin. I ask this in the wonderful name of my Lord and Savior Jesus Christ, amen.*

Step 7: Curses vs. Blessings

The next step to freedom is to renounce the sins of your ancestors as well as any curses which may have been placed on you by deceived and evil people or groups. In giving the Ten Commandments, God said,

> You shall not make for yourself an idol, or any likeness of what is in heaven above or on the earth beneath or in the water under the earth. You shall not worship them or serve them; for I, the LORD your God, am a jealous God, visiting the iniquity of the fathers on the children, on the third and the fourth generations of those who hate Me, but showing lovingkindness to thousands, to those who love Me and keep My commandments (Exodus 20:4-6).

Iniquities can be passed on from one generation to the next if you don't renounce the sins of your ancestors and claim your new spiritual heritage in Christ. You are not guilty for the sin of any ancestor, but because of his or her sin, you may be vulnerable to Satan's attack.

Because of the fall, certain strengths or weaknesses are born into you, and you are influenced by the physical and spiritual atmosphere in which you have been raised. These things can work together to cause you to struggle with a particular sin. Ask the Lord to show you specifically what sins are characteristic of your family by praying the following prayer:

> *Dear heavenly Father, I ask You to reveal to my mind now all the sins of my ancestors that are being passed down through family lines. I want to be free from those influences and walk in my new identity as a child of God. In Jesus' name, amen.*

As the Lord brings those areas of family sin to your mind, list them below. You will be specifically renouncing them later in this step.

1. _____

_____

_____

2. _____

_____

_____

3. _____

_____

_____

4. _____

_____

_____

5. _____

_____

_____

6. _____

_____

_____

7. _____

_____

_____

8. _____

_____

_____

9. _____

_____

_____

10. _____

_____

_____

In order to walk free from the sins of your ancestors and any curses and assignments targeted against you, read the following declaration and pray the following prayer out loud. Remember, you have all the authority and protection you need in Christ to take your stand against such activity.

Declaration

I here and now reject and disown all the sins of my ancestors. I specifically renounce the sins of (list here the areas of family sin the Lord revealed to you).

As one who has now been delivered from the domain of darkness into the kingdom of God's Son, I cancel out all demonic working that has been passed down to me from my family. As one who has been crucified and raised with Jesus Christ and who sits with Him in heavenly places, I renounce all satanic assignments that are directed toward me and my ministry. I cancel out every curse that Satan and his workers have put on me. I announce to Satan and all his forces that Christ became a curse for me when He died for my sins on the cross.

I reject any and every way in which Satan may claim ownership of me. I belong to the Lord Jesus Christ, who purchased me with His own blood. I reject all blood sacrifices whereby Satan may claim

*ownership of me. I declare myself to be fully and
eternally signed over and committed to the Lord
Jesus Christ.*

*By the authority I have in Christ, I now com-
mand every enemy of the Lord Jesus that is influ-
encing me to leave my presence. I commit myself to
my heavenly Father to do His will from this day forward.*

(See Galatians 3:13)

Prayer

*Dear heavenly Father, I come to You as Your child,
bought out of slavery to sin by the blood of the Lord
Jesus Christ. You are the Lord of the universe and
the Lord of my life. I submit my body to You as an
instrument of righteousness, a living and holy sacrifice, so I may glorify You in my body. I now ask
You to fill me with the Holy Spirit. I commit myself
to the renewing of my mind in order to prove that
Your will is good, acceptable, and perfect for me. All
this I pray in the name and authority of the risen
Lord Jesus Christ, amen.*

Maintaining Your Freedom

Once you have secured your freedom by going through
these seven steps, you may find demonic influences
attempting reentry days or even months later. One person
shared that she heard a spirit say to her mind "I'm back" two
days after she had been set free. "No, you're not!" she pro-
claimed aloud. The attack stopped immediately.

One victory doesn't mean that the war has been won. Freedom must be maintained. You will stay free as long as you remain in right relationship with God. If you should slip and fall, immediately get up and get right with God again.

One victim of incredible abuse shared this illustration: "Spiritual bondage is like being forced to play a game with an ugly stranger in my own home. I kept losing and I wanted to quit, but the ugly stranger wouldn't let me. Finally I called the police (a higher authority), and they came and escorted the stranger out. He knocked on the door trying to regain entry, but this time I recognized his voice and didn't let him in."

What a beautiful illustration of gaining freedom in Christ! We call upon Jesus, the highest authority in heaven and earth, and He escorts the enemy out of our lives. But it's our responsibility not to let him back in. We must know the truth, stand firm, and resist the evil one. Get involved in a church youth group and commit yourself to regular times of Bible study and prayer. God loves you, and He will never leave or forsake you.

Truth Encounter

Read:

Galatians 5:1

Reflect:

1. Finding freedom in Christ is a result of confessing, forgiving, renouncing, and forsaking. Which of these areas is the most challenging for you?

2. Is there anything you can think of that would keep you from living free in Christ today? Are there any steps you feel you need to review?

3. What steps were the most meaningful or encouraging to you? Why?

4. In what ways do you think you could share this message of freedom with others who might be struggling?

Respond:

Pray and thank God for the freedom He offers us. Also pray a prayer of commitment, that you will continue to grow and walk in freedom.

Living Free and Staying Free

FOURTEEN

THE FREEDOM YOU GAINED by walking through the Steps to Freedom in Chapter 13 must be maintained. You have won a very important battle; but the war goes on. Freedom is yours as long as you keep choosing truth and standing firm in the strength of the Lord. If old, unconfessed sins should surface, confess them. If you become aware of Satan's lies you have believed, or remember other non-Christian experiences you have had, renounce them and choose the truth. Some people have found it helpful to work through the Steps to Freedom again. As you do, follow the instructions carefully.

In this chapter we'll look at seven important Bible-based guidelines to help you maintain your freedom and walk with Christ. Be aware that we don't get any extra points with God if we follow these tips, nor do we lose points with Him if we ignore them. God loves us whether we follow His guidelines or not. However, His strong desire is that we choose to follow His guidelines and walk in freedom. Our reward for following these tips is the victory and freedom we will experience in our daily lives.

1. Strengthen Your Freedom with Fellowship

God never intended that we live the Christian life alone. That's why He created the church. Get involved with a good youth group where you can walk in the light and speak the truth in love with other growing Christians. Make sure it's a church where God's Word is taught clearly and accurately. Hebrews 10:23-25 tells us:

> Let us hold fast the confession of our hope without wavering, for He who promised is faithful; and let us consider how to stimulate one another to love and good deeds, not forsaking our own assembling together, as is the habit of some, but encouraging one another; and all the more as you see the day drawing near.

Verse 25 warns us not to forsake "our own assembling together." We are to build each other up in our faith, and that happens when we worship, pray, and study God's Word together. If we avoid going to church and meeting with other Christians, we become weak and vulnerable to the enemy's attack.

Hebrews 3:13 instructs us to "encourage one another day after day," not just on Sundays or whenever the youth group meets. We need to treat other Christians as our brothers and sisters in Christ and help one another in areas in which we need to grow.

2. Strengthen Your Freedom by Studying God's Word

The primary way to get to know God is to get to know His Word, the Bible. Reading good Christian books and listening to Christian music is great, but they are no substitute for reading and studying God's Word. There are many easy-to-read youth Bibles around for you to use. Your freedom in

Christ will really be encouraged as you get into God's Word, study it, and memorize key verses.

In the Old Testament, Ezra was a man greatly used by God. In fact, we're told that "the hand of the LORD his God was upon him" (Ezra 7:6). Ezra made God's Word a big part of his life. Verse 10 says, "Ezra had set his heart to study the law of the LORD and to practice it." Do you want God's hand on you? Set your heart to study God's Word and practice it.

It's a good idea to set a certain time each day to study your Bible and pray. If you're a "rooster" (an early-riser), the morning may be a good time for you because you're fresh and alert. If you're a "night owl" (a late-nighter), you may do better reading before you go to bed. Select a quiet, comfortable place where you won't be interrupted or distracted— but not so comfortable that you struggle to stay awake!

This special time that Christians set aside to study God's Word and pray is often called a "quiet time." Use your daily quiet time to read, study, and reflect on what God's Word has to say to you. The apostle Paul writes, "All Scripture is inspired by God and profitable for teaching, for reproof, for correction, for training in righteousness; that the man of God may be adequate, equipped for every good work" (2 Timothy 3:16,17). Therefore "be diligent to present yourself approved to God as a workman who does not need to be ashamed, handling accurately the word of truth" (2 Timothy 2:15).

3. Strengthen Your Freedom Through Daily Prayer

Proverbs 15:8 tell us, "The Lord...delights in the prayers of his people" (TLB). Because of the relationship we have with God through Christ's death, burial, and resurrection, we are free to talk to God anytime we like. And we can talk to Him about anything—friends, homework, parents, problems. Commit yourself to talk to God every day, not just during your quiet time but anytime.

Here are some sample prayers you can pray often and with confidence.

A Prayer for Daily Life

Dear heavenly Father, I honor You as my Lord. I know that You are always present with me. You are the only all-powerful, all-knowing God. You are kind and loving in all Your ways. I love You and thank You that I am united with Christ and spiritually alive in Him. I choose not to love the world, and I put to death all my sinful desires. I thank You for the life I now have in Christ, and I ask You to fill me and guide me with Your Holy Spirit so I can live my life free from sin.

I declare my dependence upon You, and I take my stand against Satan and all his lying ways. I choose to believe the truth, and I refuse to be discouraged. You are the God of all hope, and I am confident that You will meet my needs as I seek to live according to Your Word. I am confident that I can live a responsible life through Christ who strengthens me.

I now take my stand against Satan and command him and all his evil spirits to depart from me. I put on the armor of God. I submit my body as a living sacrifice and renew my mind by the living Word of God in order that I may prove that the will of God is good, acceptable, and perfect. I ask these things in the precious name of my Lord and Savior Jesus Christ, amen.

Bedtime Prayer

Thank You, Lord, that You have brought me into Your family and have blessed me with every spiritual blessing in the heavenly realm in Christ. Thank You for providing this time of rest through sleep. I accept it as part of Your perfect plan for me, and I trust You to guard my mind and my body during my sleep.

Just as I have thought on You and Your truth during this day, I also choose to let those thoughts continue in my mind while I am asleep. I commit myself to You for Your protection from every attempt of Satan or his demons to attack me during sleep. I commit myself to You as my rock, my fortress, and my resting place. I pray in the strong name of the Lord Jesus Christ, amen.

A Prayer for a Home or Room

Pray this prayer aloud after removing all articles of false worship from your room or home.

Heavenly Father, I know that You are Lord of heaven and earth. In Your power and love, You have given me all things to enjoy. Thank You for this place to live. I claim this home/room for my family/me as a place of spiritual safety and protection from all the attacks of the enemy.

As a child of God in Christ, I command all evil spirits claiming territory because of the activities of previous occupants to leave and never return. I renounce all curses and spells against this place. I ask You, heavenly Father, to post guardian angels around this home/room to guard it from the attempts of the enemy to enter and disturb Your purposes for us/me. I thank You, Lord, for doing this, and pray in the name of the Lord Jesus Christ, amen.

4. Strengthen Your Freedom by Taking Every Thought Captive

If we want to stay free in Christ, we must assume responsibility for our own thought life. Second Corinthians 10:5 instructs us to take every thought captive to the obedience of Christ. In order to remain free, we must reject the lies, choose the truth, and stand firm in our position in Christ.

Remember, we are not trying to dispel the darkness; we are trying to turn on the light. The way to overcome a lie is by choosing the truth. The way to overcome anxious thoughts is to turn to God and then do what Paul says:

> Finally, brethren, whatever is true, whatever is honorable, whatever is right, whatever is pure, whatever is lovely, whatever is of good repute, if there is any excellence and if anything worthy of praise, let your mind dwell on these things. The things you have learned and received and heard and seen in me, practice these things; and the God of peace shall be with you (Philippians 4:8,9).

If you come under direct attack, say out loud to Satan and his demons, "I command you to leave my presence in the name of the Lord Jesus Christ." Don't *ask* him to leave; *tell* him to leave in the authority of Christ: "Satan, in the name of Jesus Christ, get out of here right now." If you are paralyzed by fear and can't seem to say anything, then inwardly call upon the Lord. He knows the "thoughts and intentions of the heart" (Hebrews 4:12). Submit to God first, then resist the devil (James 4:7).

Also, keep your mind from drifting away. It's very easy to get lazy in your thinking and revert to old thought patterns. Share your struggles openly with a trusted friend or a youth leader. Paul writes, "Brethren, do not be children in your thinking; yet in evil be infants, but in your thinking be mature" (1 Corinthians 14:20).

5. Strengthen Your Freedom by Understanding Who You Are in Christ

We will grow in freedom as we continue to understand and accept our identity and worth in Christ. How can we do that? By filling our mind with the truth from God's Word about our acceptance, security, and significance in Christ.

The following statements summarize our scriptural identity and position in Christ and form the foundation for our freedom in Christ. Read these statements aloud often. Whenever you are involved in a spiritual conflict, read these statements aloud at least once each day for a month.

Who Am I?

Matthew 5:13	I am the salt of the earth
Matthew 5:14	I am the light of the world
John 1:12	I am a child of God
John 15:1,5	I am part of the true vine, and Christ's life flows through me
John 15:15	I am Christ's friend
John 15:16	I am chosen by Christ to bear fruit

Acts 1:8	I am Christ's personal witness sent out to tell everybody about Him
Romans 6:18	I am a slave of righteousness
Romans 6:22	I am a slave to God, making me holy and giving me eternal life
Romans 8:14,15; Galatians 3:26; 4:6	I am a child of God; I can call Him my Father
Romans 8:17	I am a co-heir with Christ, inheriting His glory
1 Corinthians 3:16; 6:19	I am a temple—a dwelling place—for God; His Spirit and His life live in me
1 Corinthians 6:17	I am joined forever to the Lord and am one spirit with Him
1 Corinthians 12:27	I am a part of Christ's body
2 Corinthians 5:17	I am a new person—my past is forgiven and everything is new
2 Corinthians 5:18,19	I am at peace with God, and He has given me the work of helping others find peace with Him
Galatians 3:26,28	I am a child of God and am one with others in His family
Galatians 4:6,7	I am a child of God and will receive the inheritance He has promised
Ephesians 1:1; Philippians 1:1; Colossians 1:2	I am a saint, a holy person
Ephesians 2:10	I am God's handiwork, created in Christ to do His work

Ephesians 2:19	I am a citizen of heaven along with all of God's family
Ephesians 3:1; 4:1	I am a prisoner of Christ so I can help others
Ephesians 4:24	I am righteous and holy
Philippians 3:20; Ephesians 2:6	I am a citizen of heaven seated in heaven right now
Colossians 3:3	I am hidden with Christ in God
Colossians 3:4	I am an expression of the life of Christ because He is my life
Colossians 3:12; 1 Thessalonians 1:4	I am chosen by God, holy and dearly loved
1 Thessalonians 5:5	I am a child of light and not of darkness
Hebrews 3:1	I am chosen to share in God's heavenly calling
Hebrews 3:14	I am part of Christ; I share in His life
1 Peter 2:5	I am one of God's living stones who are being built up in Christ as a spiritual house
1 Peter 2:9,10	I am a member of a chosen race, a royal priesthood, a holy nation, a people belonging to God
1 Peter 2:11	I am only a visitor to this world, in which I temporarily live
1 Peter 5:8	I am an enemy of the devil
1 John 3:1,2	I am a child of God, and I will be like Christ when He returns

1 John 5:18 .... I am born again in Christ, and the evil one—the devil—cannot touch me

Exodus 3:14;
John 8:24,28,58 .... I am *not* the great "I am,"
1 Corinthians 15:10 .... but by the grace of God, I am what I am

Since I am in Christ, by the grace of God...

Romans 5:1 .... I am now acceptable to God (justified) and completely forgiven; I live at peace with Him

Romans 6:1-7 .... The sinful person I used to be died with Christ, and sin no longer rules my life

Romans 8:1 .... I am free from the punishment (condemnation) my sin deserves

1 Corinthians 1:30 .... I have been placed into Christ by God's doing

1 Corinthians 2:12 .... I have received God's Spirit into my life; I can recognize the blessings He has given me

1 Corinthians 2:16 .... I have been given the mind of Christ; He gives me His wisdom to make right choices

1 Corinthians 6:19,20 .... I have been bought with a price; I am not my own; I belong to God

2 Corinthians 1:21,22;
Ephesians 1:13,14 .... I am God's possession, chosen and secure (sealed) in Him; I have been given the Holy Spirit as a promise of my inheritance to come

2 Corinthians 5:14,15 . . . . Since I have died, I no longer live for myself, but for Christ

2 Corinthians 5:21 . . . . I have been made acceptable to God (righteous)

Galatians 2:20 . . . . I have been crucified with Christ, and it is no longer I who live, but Christ lives in me; the life I now live is Christ's life

Ephesians 1:3 . . . . I have been blessed with every spiritual blessing

Ephesians 1:4 . . . . I was chosen in Christ to be holy before the world was created; I am without blame before Him

Ephesians 1:5 . . . . I was chosen by God (predestined) to be adopted as His child

Ephesians 1:6,7 . . . . I have been bought out of slavery to sin (redeemed) and forgiven; I have received His generous grace

Ephesians 2:5 . . . . I have been made spiritually alive just as Christ is alive

Ephesians 2:6 . . . . I have been raised up and seated with Christ in heaven

Ephesians 2:18 . . . . I have direct access to God through the Spirit

Ephesians 3:12 . . . . I may approach God with boldness, freedom, and confidence

Colossians 1:13 . . . . I have been rescued from the dark power of Satan's rule and have been brought into the kingdom of Christ

Colossians 1:14; 2:14 . . . . I have been forgiven of all my sins and set free; the debt against me has been canceled

Colossians 1:27 . . . . Christ Himself lives in me

Colossians 2:7 . . . . I am firmly rooted in Christ and am now being built up in Him

Colossians 2:10 . . . . I am fully grown (complete) in Christ

Colossians 2:12,13 . . . . I have been buried, raised, and made alive with Christ

Colossians 3:1-4 . . . . I died with Christ, and I have been raised up with Christ; my life is now hidden with Christ in God; Christ is now my life

2 Timothy 1:7 . . . . I have been given a spirit of power, love, and self-control

2 Timothy 1:9; Titus 3:5 . . . . . . I have been saved and set apart (sanctified) according to God's plan

Hebrews 2:11 . . . . Because I am set apart (sanctified) and one with Christ, He is not ashamed to call me His brother or sister

Hebrews 4:16 . . . . I have the right to come boldly before the throne of God; He will meet my needs lovingly and kindly

2 Peter 1:4 . . . . I have been given great and valuable promises; God's nature has become a part of me*

---

* Neil Anderson and Dave Park, *Stomping Out the Darkness* (Ventura, CA: Regal Books, 1993). Used by permission.

6. Strengthen Your Freedom Through Sharing Your Faith

Young people in your church and on your campus really need the Lord and the freedom He has to offer. You have the privilege and responsibility of telling others how you came to know Christ as your Savior and how you came to experience your freedom in Christ. First Peter 3:15 says, "Quietly trust yourself to Christ your Lord, and if anybody asks why you believe as you do, be ready to tell him, and do it in a gentle and respectful way" (TLB).

The strongest way to be a witness for Christ is to walk in His ways and live in His freedom. Colossians 2:6,7 tells us, "As you have received Christ Jesus the Lord, so walk in Him, having been firmly rooted and now being built up in Him and established in your faith."

You are qualified to witness and share your freedom because of who you are in Christ. You have God's Spirit and God's Word. Together, you and the Holy Spirit make a great team. Peter said in Acts 5:32, "We are witnesses of these things; and so is the Holy Spirit, whom God has given to those who obey Him." Being a successful witness is simply going to other people in the power of the Holy Spirit and confidently sharing with them the truths of the Bible through the story of how you came to know Christ and found your freedom in Him.

Pray for your non-Christian friends and those friends who have trusted Christ but are not walking in the freedom the Lord has to offer. Ask God to open doors of opportunity for you to share your faith and freedom. Remember: It's your responsibility to share, but it's the Holy Spirit's responsibility to move people's hearts to accept Christ or to make the choice to walk in His freedom. You can't fail unless you let Satan deceive you into not sharing your story.

Don't let Satan silence you through the fear of rejection or embarrassment. If you are experiencing these fears, be aware that they are not from God, because "God has not given us a spirit of timidity [fear], but of power and love and discipline" (2 Timothy 1:7). The apostle Peter puts it this way:

> And who is there to harm you if you prove zealous for what is good? But even if you should suffer for the sake of righteousness, you are blessed. And do not fear their intimidation, and do not be troubled, but sanctify [set apart] Christ as Lord in your hearts, always being ready to make a defense to everyone who asks you to give an account for the hope that is in you, yet with gentleness and reverence; and keep a good conscience (1 Peter 3:13-16).

7. Strengthen Your Freedom by Seeking Forgiveness from Others

> If you bring your gift to the altar, and there remember that your brother has something against you, leave your gift there before the altar, and go your way. First be reconciled to your brother, and then come and offer your gift. Agree with your adversary quickly, while you are on the way with him, lest your adversary deliver you to the judge, the judge hand you over to the officer, and you are thrown into prison. Assuredly, I say to you, you will by no means get out of there till you have paid the last penny (Matthew 5:23-26 NKJV).

The Motivation for Seeking Forgiveness

Matthew 5:23-26 is the key passage on seeking forgiveness. Several points in these verses are important. The worshiper coming before God to offer a gift *remembers* that someone has something against him. The Holy Spirit is the One who brings to his or her mind the wrong that was done.

Only the actions that have hurt other people need to be confessed to them. If you have had jealous, lustful, or angry thoughts toward other people and they don't know about it, these are to be confessed to God alone.

An exception to this principle occurs when restitution needs to be made. If you stole or broke something, damaged someone's reputation, and so on, you need to go to that person and make it right, even if he or she is unaware of what you did.

The Process of Seeking Forgiveness

1. Write out what you did wrong and why you did it.
2. Make sure you have already forgiven them for whatever they may have done to you.
3. Think through exactly how you will ask them to forgive you. Be sure to:
   a. Label your action as "wrong."
   b. Be specific and admit what you did.
   c. Make no defenses or excuses.
   d. Do not blame the other people, and do not expect or demand that they ask for your forgiveness.
   e. Your confession should lead to the direct question: "Will you forgive me?"
4. Look for the right place and the right time to approach the offended person.

5. Ask for forgiveness in person with anyone with whom you can talk face-to-face, with the following exception: *Do not go alone* when your safety is in danger.

6. Except where no other means of communication is possible, *do not write a letter* because a letter can be very easily misread or misunderstood; a letter can be read by the wrong people (those having nothing to do with the offense or the confession); a letter can be kept when it should have been destroyed.

7. Once you sincerely seek forgiveness, you are free—whether the other person forgives you or not (Romans 12:18).

8. After forgiveness, fellowship with God in worship (Matthew 5:24).

Truth Encounter

Read:

2 Timothy 3:15-17; Philippians 4:8,9; Hebrews 10:23-25

Reflect:

1. Why does our freedom need to be maintained? What should you do if you remember an old, unconfessed sin?

2. How does fellowship with other Christians help our walk of freedom? Why is studying God's Word so important to our freedom?

3. How is our thought life related to staying free? Why is understanding who you are in Christ so vital?

4. How did you feel after you read the "Who Am I?" list? Will anything on that list ever change?

5. What should be our motives for seeking forgiveness from other people?

Respond:

Pray and ask for God's guidance to use the authority He has given you to win the battle for your mind and to walk in freedom. Make a commitment to read the "Who Am I?" list daily and use the follow-up prayers.

A Final Encouragement

IT'S OUR HOPE THAT THROUGH this book you have met Jesus Christ the Bondage Breaker, and that through Him you have been set free. Other than eternal life, freedom in Christ is your most precious possession. It's freedom from your past. You're free to be yourself and free to grow in Christ. Jesus suffered the shame of the cross so you could be alive and free in Him, and He will always be there for you so that you can live and stay free in Him!

God has said, "Never will I leave you; never will I forsake you."
...Jesus Christ is the same yesterday and today and forever.
—HEBREWS 13:5,8 NIV

In...Christ Himself...are hidden all the treasures
of wisdom and knowledge.
—COLOSSIANS 2:2,3

If you would like to learn more about who you are in Christ and how to strengthen your walk with God, then check out these great books:

The Bondage Breaker Youth Edition Study Guide by Neil Anderson and Dave Park

Stomping Out the Darkness by Neil Anderson and Dave Park

Stomping Out the Darkness Study Guide by Neil Anderson and Dave Park

Busting Free Youth Curriculum by Dave Park

Busting Free Video Series by Dave Park

FREEDOM IN CHRIST 4 TEENS

Higher Ground by Neil Anderson, Robert Saucy, and Dave Park

Purity Under Pressure by Neil Anderson and Dave Park

DEVOTIONAL SERIES

Extreme Faith by Neil Anderson and Dave Park

Reality Check by Neil Anderson and Rich Miller

Awesome God by Neil Anderson and Rich Miller

Ultimate Love by Neil Anderson and Dave Park

Righteous Pursuit by Neil Anderson and Dave Park

Freedom in Christ Youth Ministries

Freedom in Christ Youth Ministries offers conferences! See the list below and contact us for more information.

If you're a youth worker and would like to become certified to conduct a Stomping Out the Darkness student conference for your youth, call us today at 623-925-5555.

For more information about Freedom in Christ Youth Ministries or the resources they have to offer, or to have Dave Park speak at your church, please write or call:

Freedom in Christ Youth Ministries
9051 Executive Park Dr., Suite 503
Knoxville, TN 37923
865-342-4000 Phone
865-342-4001 Fax
E-mail: dave@ficm.org
Website: www.ficyouth.com

Youth Conferences from FIC Student Ministries

Stomping Out the Darkness
Find out who you are in Christ and why you don't have to put up with the world's garbage anymore.

Purity Under Pressure Student Conference on Sexual Purity
Learn how to stand for purity even when you're under pressure.

Total Abandon Student Prayer Conference
Learning to call on His name and experiencing God's awesome presence and incredible power through prayer.

Awesome God Life of Christ Conference

Discover the richness of the life of Christ and how His life can change your life.

Parent Conferences from FIC Student Ministries

Setting Your Home Free: The Seduction of Our Teens

Understanding today's youth and setting them free.

Youth Worker Conferences from FIC Student Ministries

Setting Your Youth Free: Spiritual Conflicts and Counseling Youth

Practical and biblical answers to help youth find freedom in Christ, along with guidelines on establishing a freedom ministry in your church.

Freedom in Christ Ministries

Freedom in Christ is an international ministry which exists to glorify God by equipping churches, Christian organizations, and mission groups in obedience to the Great Commandment in order to accomplish the Great Commission.

Thousands have found their freedom in Christ; your group can too! Here are some conferences you can host, led by Freedom in Christ staff, that can change your community:

Living Free in Christ
A Bible conference on resolving personal and spiritual conflicts
Discipleship Counseling
A two-day advanced seminar on helping others find freedom in Christ
Setting Your Church Free
A leadership conference on corporate freedom for churches, ministries, or mission groups
*Resolving Spiritual Conflicts and
Cross-Cultural Ministry*
A conference for leaders, missionaries, and all believers desiring to see the Great Commission fulfilled
Setting Your Marriage Free
A two-day event for engaged couples, newlyweds, or those who have been married many years

The above conferences are also available on video- and audiocassettes, except for *Setting Your Marriage Free*. To order these and other resources, write or call us at the address below.

To host a conference, feel free to contact us:
Freedom in Christ
9051 Executive Park Dr., Suite 503
Knoxville, TN 37923
865-342-4000 Phone
865-342-4001 Fax
E-mail: dave@ficm.org
Website: www.ficm.org

More books from Neil Anderson to help you and those you love find freedom in Christ.

- *Victory Over the Darkness*
  Regal Books
- *The Bondage Breaker*
  Harvest House Publishers
- *The Bondage Breaker Audiobook*
  Harvest House Publishers
- *The Bondage Breaker Study Guide*
  Harvest House Publishers
- *Spiritual Warfare* (with Timothy M. Warner)
  Crossway Books
- *Walking in the Light*
  Thomas Nelson Publishers
- *The Seduction of Our Children* (with Steve Russo)
  Harvest House Publishers
- *Released from Bondage*
  Thomas Nelson Publishers
- *Breaking Through to Spiritual Maturity*
  Regal Books
- *Living Free in Christ*
  Regal Books
- *God's Power at Work in You* (with Robert Saucy)
  Harvest House Publishers
- *Freedom from Fear* (with Rich Miller)
  Harvest House Publishers
- *A Way of Escape*
  Harvest House Publishers
- *Daily in Christ* (with Joanne Anderson)
  Harvest House Publishers

To find out more, please write or call us at
FREEDOM IN CHRIST MINISTRIES
9051 Executive Park Dr., Suite 503 • Knoxville, TN 37923
Phone: 865-342-4000 • Fax: 865-342-4001
E-mail: info@ficm.org
Website: www.ficm.org